STUDIO TIPS

for artists & graphic designers

BILL GRAY

LUND HUMPHRIES • LONDON

To Stacey, with love

Published in Great Britain in 1989 by
Lund Humphries Publishers Ltd
16 Pembridge Road London W11 3HL

British Library Cataloguing in Publication Data
Gray, Bill
    Studio tips for artists and graphic designers
    1. Graphic arts. Manuals
    I. Title
    760'.028

ISBN 0 85331 562 0

Printed in Great Britain by
The Camelot Press, Southampton

Contents

Foreword

The writer has just celebrated his fiftieth year as a graphic artist. During this time many new ways and shortcuts were found to help solve graphic art problems. These helpful hints and tips are accumulated here to make the information immediately available to all graphic artists, whether they be students or old pros. I know that in many cases application of one or more of these tips will not only solve a problem but will save time and money as well.

If your day-to-day work as a graphic artist is made easier from following these suggestions, the purpose of writing this book will have been accomplished.

Grateful acknowledgment is given herewith to my editors for their suggestions. My special thanks go to Miss Estelle Silbermann, who was most helpful in making crystal clear many of the descriptions.

How to check the trueness of your drawing board and triangles

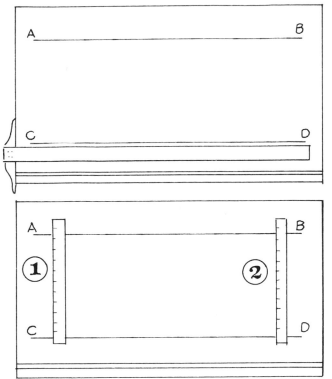

With your Tsquare head snug against the left edge of the drawing board, draw line AB, then line CD, relatively far apart.

Remove the Tsquare. _Carefully_ measure the distance at left ①, and distance at right ②, between the two parallel lines. They should be _exactly_ the same distance. If they are, your Tsquare and drawing board are "en rapport."

Holding the Tsquare snugly against the left edge of the drawing board, and with your triangle in the un-normal position, draw line AB. Flip the triangle to its normal position (dotted lines) and draw line AB. The two lines should be _exactly_ the same line. Check all sides of all triangles in a similar manner.

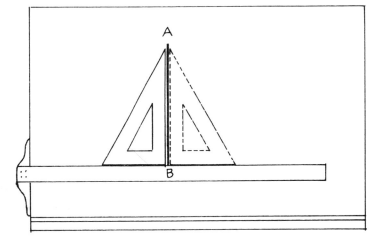

How to position art on the drawing board

Art, or a mechanical paste-up, should be positioned toward the left side of your drawing board and should be close to the head of your T square as shown

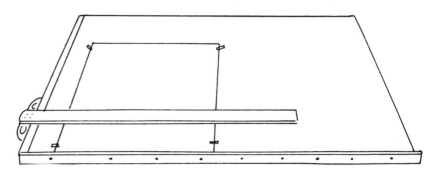

here. In this way there will be less of a chance for making errors since you will be able to control your T square much more easily and lines that you draw with the T square and triangles will be much more accurate.

How to prevent things from sliding off the drawing board

A large piece of sandpaper can be rubber cemented to the right side of your drawing board, as shown, to prevent tools and other objects from sliding down the board and falling on the floor.

Attach a thin strip to the bottom of the drawing board. Jars, pencils, brushes, etc., will then not slide off the board onto the floor. It is also great for resting art work against when erasing.

Glue strips of sandpaper on bottoms of bottles, rulers, and other things that slide easily.

How to draw over the edge of your drawing board

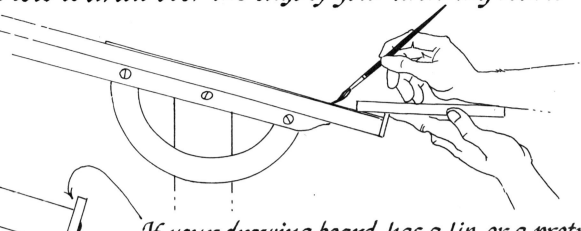

If your drawing board has a lip or a protruding edge at its lower side, it may be uncomfortable to draw near this edge. If you have this difficulty hold a thin board over the edge as a hand rest; a small tracing pad or other flat object may do.

There may be other situations where the use of a small flat piece as a hand rest can be helpful.

How to prevent ink or any other bottles from tipping over

← Cut a strip of paper about 6" x 1".

Cut a slit in the paper, as shown. Where the neck of the bottle appears cut a small opening. Attach the paper strip to your drawing board with pins or tape.

The assembly can be attached to a small heavy card and moved.

CAN BE USED ON ALL TYPES OF BOTTLES.

INK

How to make a "clothesline" file

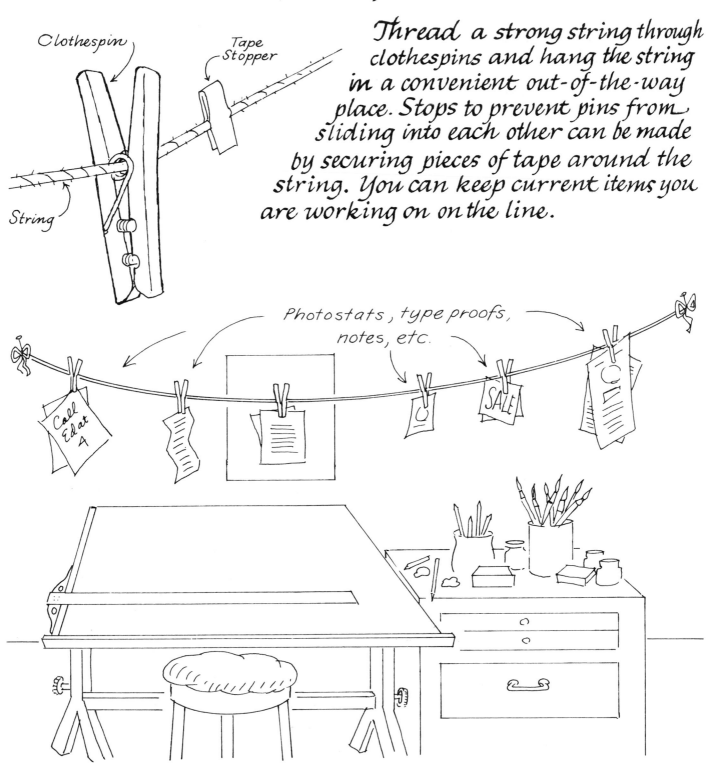

Clothespin

Tape Stopper

String

Thread a strong string through clothespins and hang the string in a convenient out-of-the-way place. Stops to prevent pins from sliding into each other can be made by securing pieces of tape around the string. You can keep current items you are working on on the line.

Photostats, type proofs, notes, etc.

Call Ed at 4

SALE

How to prevent stacked pieces from sliding

First cut a stiff card and fold as shown.

7" APPROX.

3"

Shape a "stopper" and secure to table top or floor with tape or pins.

Use on table or other top.

A small block of wood could be nailed or glued to the floor for a more permanent "stopper."

Many cards, boards, and other objects can be leaned against the wall and will not slide to the floor with this expedient temporary method.

How to make your drawing table, chair, and other furniture pieces slide more easily

If you have trouble moving your drawing board and other studio furniture...

Furniture slides

...buy some furniture slides (at any hardware store) and, turning the furniture upside down, nail the slides into the bottom legs. The furniture will then slide much more easily.

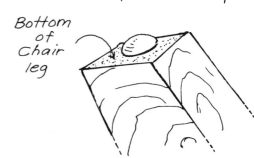

Bottom of chair leg

How to prevent knocking things off the board with your T square

If you are one of those artists (I am) who sometimes works with a cluttered drawing board and you are constantly knocking items to the floor, draw a heavy line at the extreme limits of your T square and to the right of your working area. This line acts as a boundary. Never put any items to the left of it, where they would interfere with the action of your T square or get knocked down.

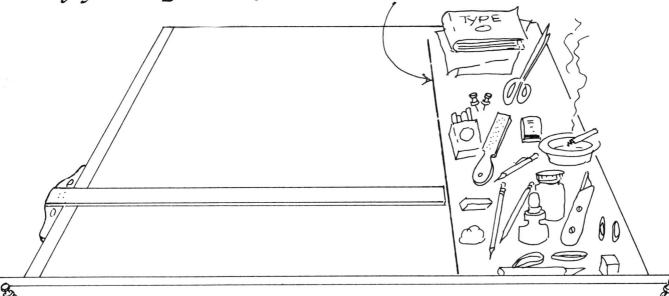

How always to have a pen wiper and wipe rag handy

A piece of cheesecloth can be hung at each end of your drawing board so that the cloth can be used conveniently at either side for wiping pens, pointed pencils, or other tools. The cheesecloth pieces can be washed daily — or whenever necessary. Washed cheesecloth is more absorbent than most other rag material. Wring the rags out at the sink and they will dry while hanging.

Handlling Art Work

Keep thumbs off the art work.

Always hold the art by the sides, as shown.

Never talk, cough, or sneeze over art, especially when the art is flat, airbrushed and unflapped. Drink your coffee, tea, or anything else, away from the art.

Please return to
GARY SAMPLE
211 MARKET ST.
RIVERVIEW, O.
33106

How to minimize loss of your art work.

On the back of every piece of art work (photographs, drawings, and other art) that belongs to you should be your complete name and address. This will minimize any chance of losing the art in transit to the printer, or wherever it is going. A rubber stamp may save you time.

How to mail art work

Lay 2 oversized pieces of corrugated boards (bigger than the art work) over the art, as shown. The corrugated boards are at right angles to each other to minimize the possibility of your package getting bent. Wrap well and put addresses on <u>both</u> sides of the package. Insure and send.

For extra insurance against bending, you can double the pieces, always at right angles to each other.

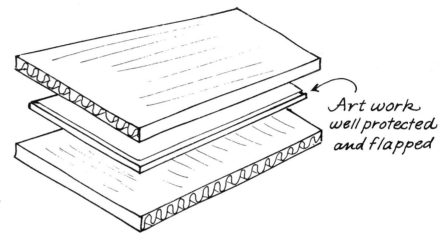

Art work well protected and flapped

Never lay anything on top of flat art work

even if it does have a flap to protect it.

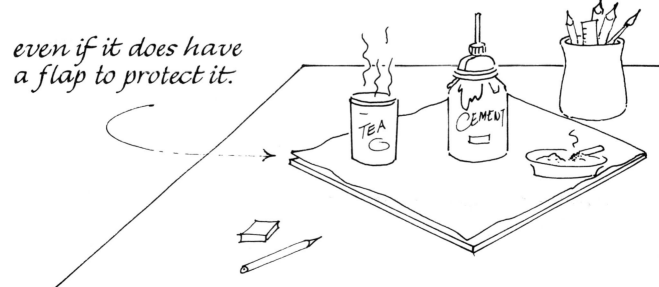

How to make a "sandpaper layout"

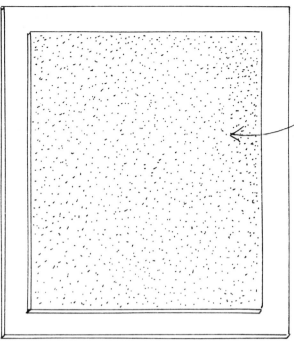

As an aid in developing a layout, you can use the sandpaper technique described here.

First, rubber cement a piece of sandpaper to a piece of illustration board. The size of the sandpaper should be exactly the same as the size of your layout.

On the backs of all your elements (type, logos, illustrations, or anything else), paste small strips of sandpaper.

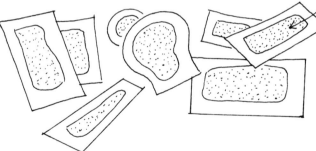

You can then move the pieces around on the large board until you get a satisfactory arrangement.

The sandpaper-backed pieces will adhere readily to the large piece of sandpaper.

Finished layout

How to make an acetate overlay on a mechanical

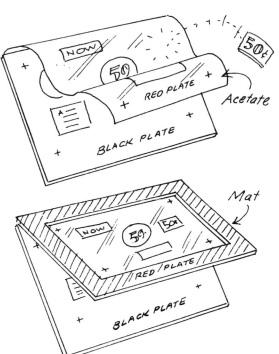

Sometimes you may have a flexible acetate overlay on a mechanical upon which you paste other items which then sometimes flip off as the mechanical is moved around.

To prevent, or minimize, the possibility of these items flipping off, prepare a stiff board mat (made of card) for the acetate. This mat will hinge rigidly on the mechanical and not bend so that items pasted down will have a better chance of staying on.

How to make a color overlay on a mechanical

If you have a mechanical paste-up with many elements cemented thereon which are thick and heavy or of varying weights, the job of making a tissue overlay for color break, or other reasons, will be much simpler if, before any indications are made on the overlay, you insert a piece of heavy acetate between the mechanical and the tissue.

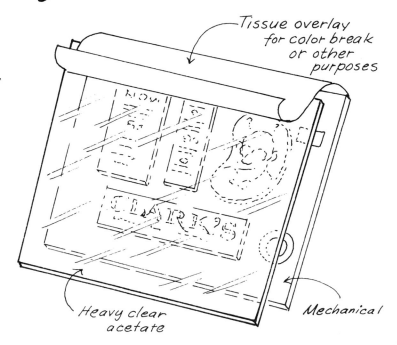

How to be sure your mechanical paste-up has no excess cement

If you have been missing too many rubber cement spots on your mechanicals that should have been cleaned off, hold your paste-up to a light and you will be able to see easily any excess rubber cement you missed in cleaning up. You can also hold the mechanical to the window light; just move it around and you will see the neglected spots.

How to use an old telephone book as an aid in paste-up

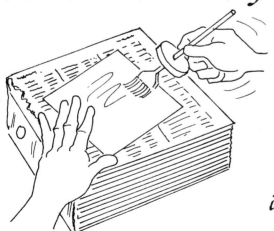

An old telephone book, or a similar catalogue, is great as a back up for brushing rubber cement on things to be pasted up on mechanicals or other surfaces. After using the top page, it can be discarded, and then the next clean page is ready for use.

A pile of newspaper pages is also a handy item to have around for a similar purpose.

How to avoid cut marks on stats when making a negative paste-up

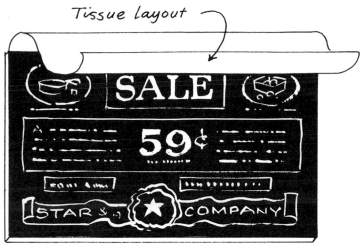

Tissue layout

The negative paste-up. All negative black photostats have been pasted in position onto a black cardboard.

Negative stat

Tweezers

If you paste up many negative photostats or prints onto a black background (whether it is card, paper, or any other material), you should paint the edges black on every negative print before pasting it down. Otherwise the cut edges, being white on the negative paste-up, will be black marks on the positive print that you get back from the photostatter.

Waterproof black ink should be applied to the white edges of all the negative photostats with a brush, as shown, before pasting them in position on the black card.

First paste rubber cement on the backs of all stats. Next, trim them close to the images, and then paint with black ink. Apply rubber cement over the entire area of the black card. Flap a tissue layout over this card so that you can position the stats exactly where you want them when you paste them down.

How to paste down wrinkled art work

Suppose that you designed a layout on tracing paper which, for some reason, was discarded. Now that you want to present it, it is a wrinkled mass. Here is what you can do.

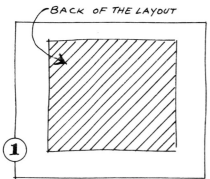

① BACK OF THE LAYOUT

② POSITION FOR TOP OF LAYOUT

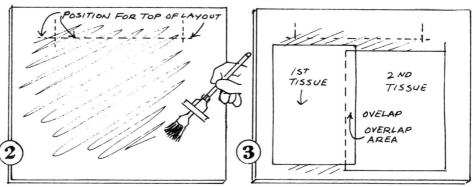

③ 1ST TISSUE / 2ND TISSUE / OVELAP / OVERLAP AREA

Carefully unravel the layout and coat the back with rubber cement ①. Rubber cement the board to which you are going to adhere the layout after marking the position for the top of the layout. ②. Over the cemented board, lay 2 pieces of tracing paper that overlap slightly ③, just below the mark for the top of the layout.

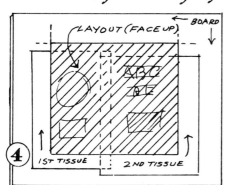

④ LAYOUT (FACE UP) / BOARD / 1ST TISSUE / 2ND TISSUE

⑤

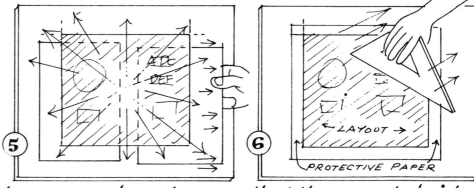

⑥ LAYOUT / PROTECTIVE PAPER

In this overlap area, turn your layout over so that the cemented side is down ④. Lay still another piece of tracing paper over the entire area (to protect it) and iron the layout to the board with your hand, always applying pressure from the center out to the edges (arrows) ⑤. Now gradually, one at a time, slip the sheets away ⑤. Finally, over tracing paper, iron the layout to the board with the edge of a triangle ⑥. Clean and trim the layout.

How to dry mount and wet mount with rubber cement
Dry mount

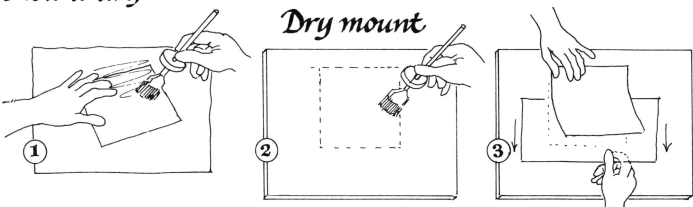

Place the piece to be pasted face down on a clean surface. Spread rubber cement over the back ①. Then spread rubber cement over the area of the mechanical (dotted line) where the piece is to be positioned ②. When both cemented areas are dry, _carefully_ set the rubber-cemented piece in place on the mechanical and apply pressure. A piece of clean tracing paper can be placed under the piece before applying pressure and withdrawn slowly as you dry mount the piece to the mechanical ③.

Wet mount

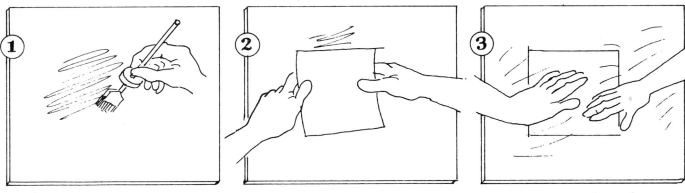

First, put rubber cement on the area which will receive the piece to be pasted onto the mechanical ①. Next, position the piece, laying it down flat – move it around until it is in the exact position you want ②. Then apply pressure over all. Work relatively fast in the wet method ③. Try to position the piece while the rubber cement is wet. In the dry mount method at top, take all the time you want.

Tips on making a mechanical

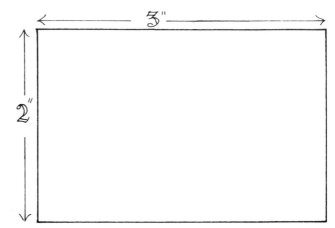

When drawing a dotted-line box, be sure that corners meet, as in B — never as in A.

Always give measurements width first, then height. For example, the above rectangle is 3" x 2".

Mechanical paste-up

To be certain that the printer does not make a plate of the photos in paste-ups, draw an "X" in ink through the photostats of tone art being used for positioning on the mechanical.

If a bubble appears on a pasted-down piece, prick the bubble with a push-pin or a knife point and let the air out. Then press down flat around the spot. A strategic slit with a stencil knife may also do the trick. Be careful not to damage the art work, however.

How to paste up a large photostat on a mechanical

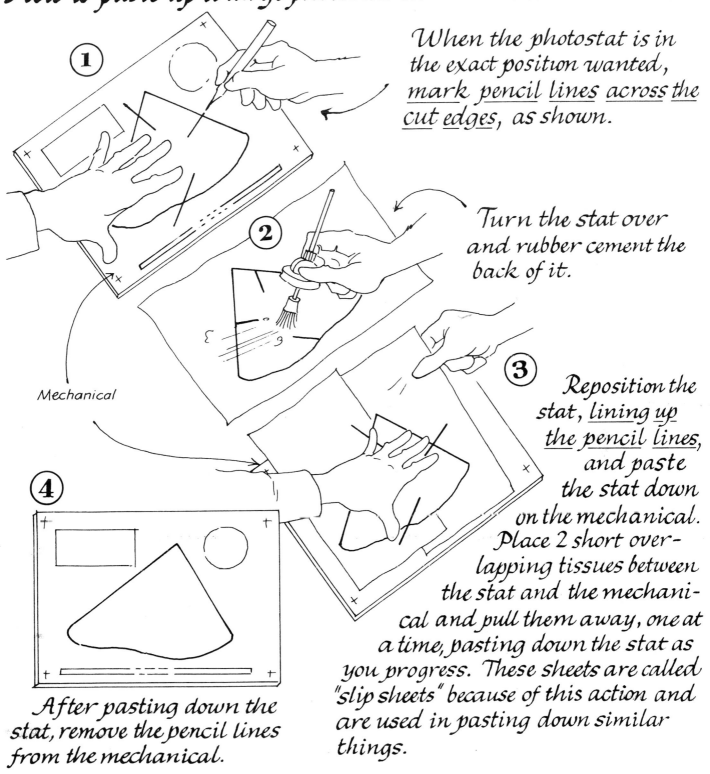

When the photostat is in the exact position wanted, <u>mark pencil lines across the cut edges</u>, as shown.

Turn the stat over and rubber cement the back of it.

Mechanical

Reposition the stat, <u>lining up the pencil lines</u>, and paste the stat down on the mechanical. Place 2 short overlapping tissues between the stat and the mechanical and pull them away, one at a time, pasting down the stat as you progress. These sheets are called "slip sheets" because of this action and are used in pasting down similar things.

After pasting down the stat, remove the pencil lines from the mechanical.

How to keep your layout pad and tissue sheets from moving

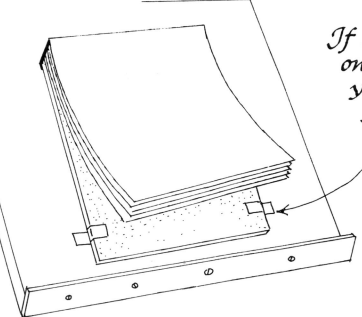

If your layout pad moves on the drawing board as you draw on it, attach small strips of tape to the pad backing and to the board.

If the tissue sheets of the pad move ...

...attach strips of tape around all of the sheets to bind them all together. As you need new sheets to work on, pick the tape from the top sheet with a fingernail, lift and remove the sheet you have just worked on, then re-attach the tape.

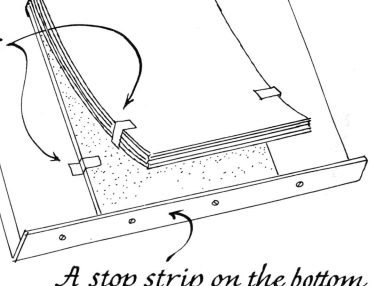

A stop strip on the bottom of the drawing board is great for resting the pad against.

Photographs and Photographic Techniques
How to work with photographs

Never write instructions on the back of a photograph – especially not with a hard ball-point pen ...

... or a marker pen. The ink of a marker pen may bleed through and stain the photo on the other side.

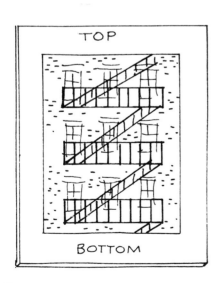

A stabilo pencil is made especially for writing on glossy surfaces.

Always mark TOP and BOTTOM on all photos, particularly on photos in which the subject is not easily recognized.

Always ask for margins on photos where you can mark instructions.

How to order photostats

A photostat is an inexpensive photographic image usually done on cheap photostat paper. _Glossy_ photostats are normally ordered for line art and <u>mat</u> for continuous tone art. If you have your own photostat-machine, you can set your own system for ordering them. Most photostat companies prefer the labelling shown below.*

* usage more common in USA

3 separate different pieces of original art }

Order a **first print** if you want this }

Order a **second print** if you want this }

Unless you have an arrangement with your photostat company, do not use terms like negative, positive, and opposite.

Do not use marker pens for writing instructions on a photostat. They may bleed through and spoil the print.

When giving sizes for enlargements or reductions, use percentages instead of linear measurements because percentages are much more accurate. Use a proportion scale for this purpose.

Always write your name and company on every photostat

A sample instruction looks like this →

1 Glossy 2nd print at 54%
Jonathan Thompson
Beejay Company

How to "gang-up" photostats and save money

When ordering photostats, use up all the space that you are paying for in the print you will get back. Check the sizes and prices of prints with your photostatter.

Put as many images on your original copy as you can within the limits of the stat size you will get back. This method of putting more than 1 image on your original is called "ganging-up".

Original marked-up Copy

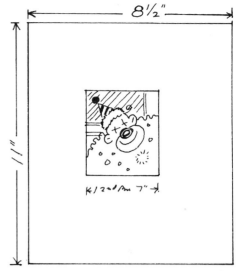

Photostat, as ordered. Wasted space could have been used for other stat material.

Original marked-up copy correctly filled

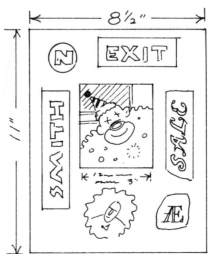

Photostat of your original, with no wasted space

Fill up all of the space you are paying for with all kind of useable items (such as logos, for example) in addition to the illustrations.

How to retouch a photograph with laundry bleach

Photo, before retouching

Swabbing bleach on the area to be removed.

Photograph after the un-wanted area is removed.

Ordinary household bleach

Q-tips

Bleach

Container

Household bleach can be used on photographs and photostats (line or continuous tone art) to bleach out unwanted areas or lines and return the retouched area to absolute white of the print. Use a Q-tip or a cotton ball as a swab. Apply the bleach by gently rubbing the image to be eliminated. Blotters should be kept handy to help dry the wet area.

How to make a 3-D design photographically

If you want a repeated element in a design, such as the one to the right, you can accomplish this in a simple photographic way by first lettering the elementary design horizontally

When the lettering is finished, attach it, as shown, to a large cardboard tube or cylinder. Give the photographer or photostatter a focal point where he is to center his lens. If you want the design to curve down, the focal point on the cylinder is above the design as in ①. If you want it to curve up, the focal point is below as in ②.

A strip of 5 vertical designs can be photographed 2 times, for example, and finally assembled in the form shown at the top.

The design can be attached on the tube in different positions from the one shown. Try some of your own.

How to make a filmstrip of your own alphabet

If you have a photo-composing machine that can use a 2"-high filmstrip, you can make your own alphabet for use thereon.

ORIGINAL ART

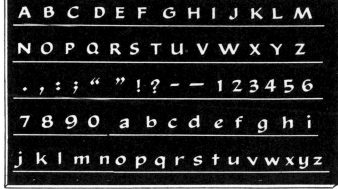

SAME SIZE FILM NEGATIVE FROM THE PRINTER

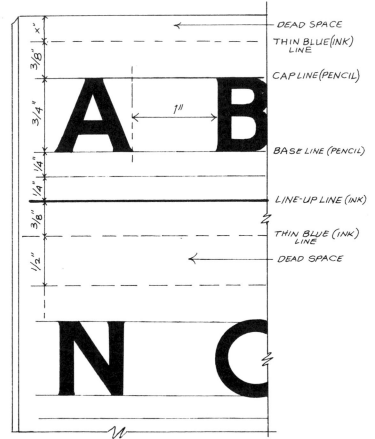

ENLARGED VIEW OF UPPER LEFT CORNER OF ORIGINAL ART

First design your alphabet. The letters must be positioned as shown in the enlarged diagram at left. The dotted lines indicate thin solid blue lines and will not appear on the film negative — they are drawn to help you organize the letters on the art.

Note _all_ dimensions.

The line-up line must be exactly 1/4" from the drop line for ALL characters. The height of the capitals can be less than, but no more than, 3/4".

Because of the mechanical requirements of photo-composing, the letters must be spaced at least 1" apart horizontally.

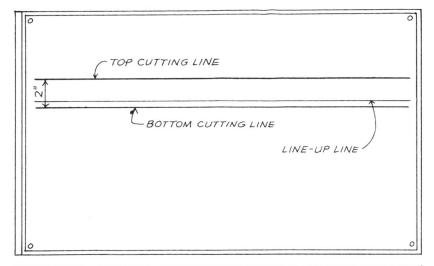

TOP CUTTING LINE

2"

BOTTOM CUTTING LINE

LINE-UP LINE

1ST 2" STRIP CUT

A B C D E F G H I J K L M

2ND STRIP READY TO BE CUT

N O P Q R S T U V W X Y Z

←PIN   PIN→

. , ; ' ! ? — — 1 2 3 4 5 6

7 8 9 0 a b c d e f g h i j

k l m n o p q r s t u v w x y z

SCOTCH TAPE

H I J K L M   N O P Q R S

ALIGN THE STRIPS TOP AND BOTTOM WITH A T SQUARE,
JOIN THEM WITH SCOTCH TAPE ON BOTH SIDES

When you get the complete film negative, cut it into 2"-high strips, as shown here. Attach a clean white card, larger than the negative, to your drawing board. Draw 2 thin black ink lines exactly 2" apart. Then draw the line-up line in a heavier black line with the same relation to the other lines as shown on the opposite page. Attach your film to another white card and trim it close to the edges. Now, line up the line-up line with a long metal Tsquare and attach the film card to your board. Cut the film on both lines 2" apart on your drawing board. Use pushpins against the bottom of the Tsquare so that it will not move as you cut. Raise the film card, align your Tsquare with a new line-up line and repeat the procedure. When all the strips are cut, join them with thin scotch tape as shown, starting with the last 2 strips. Work in the reverse alphabet order, gathering the completed strip to the right. The strips must be checked, top and bottom, to insure a good alignment of the edges. Retouch all marks on a light box. Attach the completed strip to a reel and use in your machine.

How to prepare a photograph for the printer

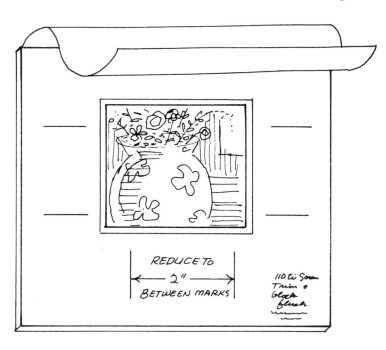

REDUCE TO
2"
BETWEEN MARKS

Always carefully dry mount photographs on heavy card or illustration board, leaving wide borders, as shown. The card must have a flap that acts as a protective covering.

Specifications to the printer are written on the card's borders or on a tissue flap over the photograph—__never__ directly on the photograph. If you give instructions on the tissue overlay, be sure the photo's surface is protected by a piece of heavy acetate before you start writing.

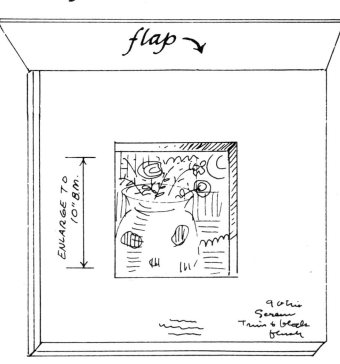

flap

ENLARGE TO 10" 8m.

If you have a retouched photograph or expensive or delicate art, make a heavy mat, thick enough to protect the face of the art. A __heavy__ cardboard flap should be taped to the top and hinge over the art.

Working with Acetate and Other Surfaces
How to paste a print on a glossy photo

Sometimes when you rubber cement a print to a photograph or photostat — especially a glossy photo — it will not stay adhered.

If you have this trouble...

WHITE TEMPERA

...paint the area to be pasted with white paint.

When the paint is dry, paste the piece on. It should now stay on.

How to draw difficult subjects on acetate or glass

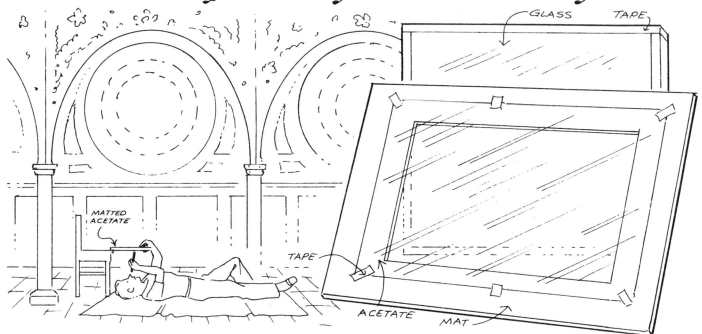

There may be an occasion when it is necessary to draw a complicated subject and you do not have much time. Unusual perspective views, very complicated pieces of machinery, or a cluttered scene with unusual architecture are some possible examples of such subjects. Many times an artist will use a camera in these situations and later enlarge the picture and use it for reference. As a substitute you can, however, use a piece of acetate taped to a heavy mat, hold it steadily at the desired position, and make a quick sketch with a felt-nib pen. A piece of glass, heavily taped on the edges for safety, can be used in the same manner. When you return to the studio, the back of the acetate or glass can be painted white and, when dry, can be photostatted for a larger or smaller print — as desired.

As you sketch the subject, your head must remain still. You can see better, sharper images if you keep one eye closed as well.

How to use acetate to trace a drawing from a continuous-tone photo

If you want to reduce a continuous-tone photo or picture from a magazine or other source to a piece of line art...

Photo

Acetate

...lay a piece of acetate over the photo and draw an inked line-art drawing with a pen or brush.

If desired, corrections — such as things you want left out, for example — can be made as you progress with the line drawing. When you are finished, turn over the acetate and paint the back with white paint. You can send out to get a clean, sharp photostat, which can be enlarged, reduced, or the same size.

White

Back of acetate

How to make watercolor stick to shiny surfaces

Shown here are 3 ways to help water-soluble paint stay on shiny surfaces such as acetate, glass, foil cards, and other shiny surfaces.

If you have trouble keeping water-soluble color adhered, especially for large color areas, mix a little casein glue with tempera, poster color, or other paint and you will find that the paint never comes off.

You must work reasonably fast or the casein may dry up before you are finished with it.

Mucilage can be mixed with the water-soluble paint before using. A small amount of oxgall mixed with the paint is also good.

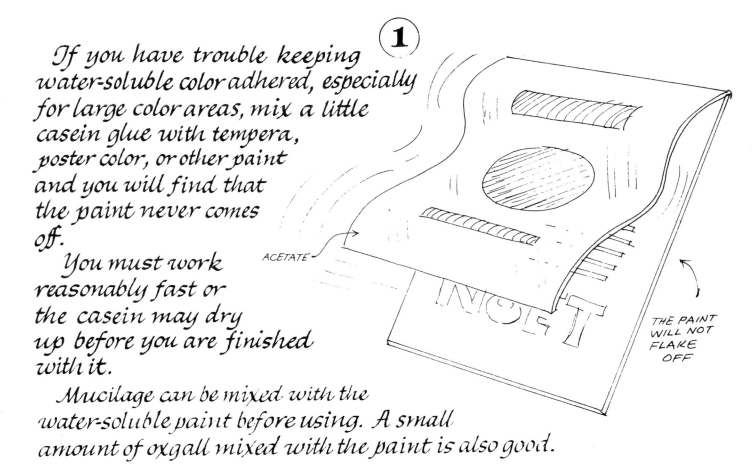

ACETATE

THE PAINT WILL NOT FLAKE OFF

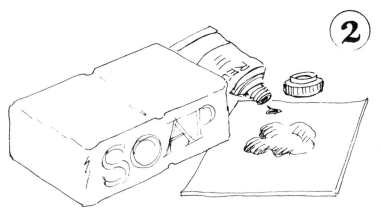

A little soap mixed with the water-soluble paint helps it lay flat and adhere to glossy surfaces. A little saliva has the same effect.

③

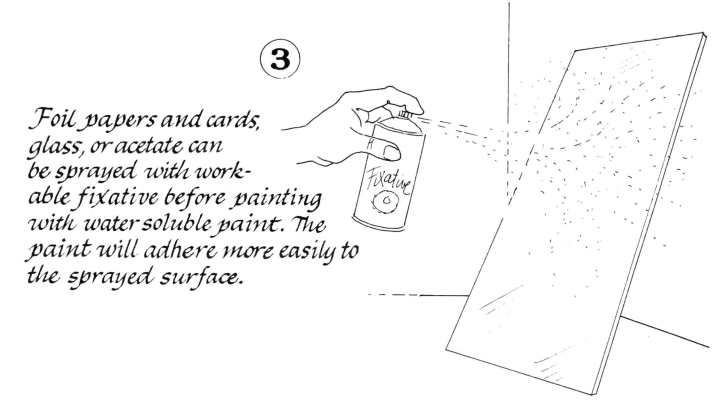

Foil papers and cards, glass, or acetate can be sprayed with workable fixative before painting with water soluble paint. The paint will adhere more easily to the sprayed surface.

How to paint with watercolor on a wax surface

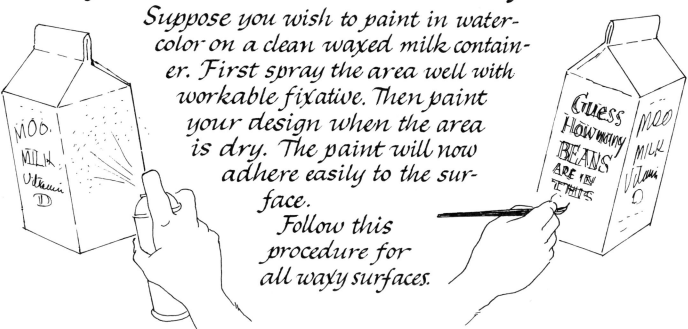

Suppose you wish to paint in watercolor on a clean waxed milk container. First spray the area well with workable fixative. Then paint your design when the area is dry. The paint will now adhere easily to the surface.

Follow this procedure for all waxy surfaces.

Type
How to "fix" type proofs

The quick brown fox jumps over the lazy dog

Ace #1 ⊕ TYPOGRAPHY
SHEET 3461
MAY 11 14

Pastel Fixative

If you "fix" type proofs for future use or if they are "wet", do not spray the proofs with pastel fixative — they will run.

Spray with one of the gloss sprays.

Do not "overspray" or hold at one spot too long.

Gloss

Gloss

The quick brown fox jumps over the lazy dog.

Ace #1 ⊕ TYPOGRAPHY
SHEET 3461
MAY...

Spray with an up-and-down motion, at least 12" away from the proofs, as with any other spray.

How to paste down type on a curved alignment

In pencil, draw the curve on which you desire to position the type on your mechanical.

Trace this curve on a piece of tracing paper, lay it over the type proof and trace the letters, turning the paper frequently to have the letters align on the curve as you want. You should have a tracing that looks like this, when finished.

Trim the type line close at the top and bottom and, by inspection, slit with a sharp knife from the edges in (shown below with dotted lines) according to how the letters turn. Attach the tracing to the mechan-

THE QUICK BROWN FOX JUMPS OVER THE MOON

ical, matching the curves, and use it as a guide. Apply rubber cement to the back of the sliced type proof and also to the curved line on the mechanical. Use a tissue slip sheet under the proof as you dry mount it down along the curve. A pair of tweezers will help. When you are finished cementing the proof down, clean up and...

THE QUICK BROWN FOX JUMPS OVER THE MOON

...what you have should look something like this

How to indicate small type on a layout

When you squint your eyes and look at a column of type you see lines of body — all lower-case letters have a body, but not all have ascenders and descenders. So the body is what you indicate to give a good impression of the type on a layout.

Sometimes the body is indicated with a solid line and sometimes 2 lines — the top line for the waist line and the bottom line for the base line.

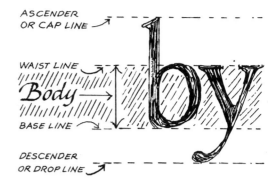

ASCENDER OR CAP LINE

WAIST LINE

Body

BASE LINE

DESCENDER OR DROP LINE

The body of the type — the dark area above — is the part that you indicate.

Single stroke of pencil or other tool

Neat, ruled double lines for each line of type

Scratchy single stroke with breaks here and there

Scratchy double lines broken to indicate words here and there

Wiggly scribbles to simulate words. The squiggles are broken here and there and an aligning line may be indicated.

Nonreading letters (greeking) can be sketched in with aligning waist and base lines. The weight of the type is indicated in the letters.

38

Length-of-line and leading tables

A beginner designing typographic text copy should adhere to time-tested rules for length of line and leading (the space between lines) in order to achieve maximum readability of the text – which is, after all, the primary aim of all good typography. Shown below are accepted standards for accomplishing this maximum legibility. As the designer's experience widens he may vary these requirements for artistic effect, but this does not alter the legibility rules.

Length-of-line table

TYPE SIZE	MINIMUM LENGTH	MAXIMUM LENGTH
6 point	8 picas	10 picas
8 "	9 "	13 "
10 "	13 "	16 "
11 "	13 "	18 "
12 "	14 "	21 "
14 "	18 "	24 "
18 "	24 "	30 "

Leading table

TYPE SIZE	MINIMUM LEADING	MAXIMUM LEADING
6 point	Solid (no lead)	1 point
8 "	"	2 "
10 "	Solid to 2 point	4 "
11 "	1 point	4 "
12 "	2 "	6 "
14 "	3 "	8 "

Since there are 72 points to 1 inch and 6 picas to 1 inch, therefore 12 points equal 1 pica. For type sizes larger than those given, use your own judgment.

How to copyfit – from text (manuscript) to type proof

Layout
TEXT

8½"
5½"

Manuscript
TEXT IS DOUBLE-SPACED WHEN TYPEWRITTEN.

TYPE SPECIMENS
ALL STYLES
— & —
SIZES
ABC Type Co.

Type specimen book

Pica ruler

TYPE FACES	SIZES				
	10	11	12	14	16
CENTURY EXPANDED	2.6	2.4	2.2	1.8	1.
FUTURA BOOK	3.0	2.7	2.5	2.3	2
GARAMOND	2.9	2.7	2.6	2.3	2.
NEWS GOTHIC	2.4	2.7	2.3	1.9	
TIMES ROMAN	2.8	2.5	2.3	2.1	1.

Characters-per-pica chart. THESE ARE FOUND IN MOST SPECIMEN BOOKS.

The most accurate system for copyfitting is based on character count. The following step-by-step sequence is necessary in using this system. The "tools" you will need are shown above.

① Get a total count of all the characters in your manuscript. Count one each for small letters, word space, and punctuation mark, 2 for each cap.

② Select a type style and size from your specimen book.

③ In picas, measure the width of a line on your layout. Avoid fractions if you can – it will make your arithmetic easier.

④ Find how many characters of your chosen type face will fit this one line measure. Calculate it from your characters-per-pica chart.

⑤ Divide the number of characters in one line into the total count of the entire manuscript to find the total number of lines required.

⑥ Multiply the number of lines by the point size of your type and you will get the total depth (in points) for your manuscript.

⑦ Add leading (nonprinting space between lines) if desired, and check the new depth with your layout.

⑧ If this final depth doesn't fit your layout, you can change the layout, or change your type size, or the leading, or all of these, and calculate the entire program again – until the type fits your layout.

⑨ Mark up the manuscript (specs) for the type composition.

● Remember that 12 points = 1 pica, 6 picas = 1 inch, and 72 points = 1 inch.

The Manuscript

|← ——————— 40 characters ——————— →|

```
Then suddenly, out of the storm there appeared... a reindeer!

It leaped and pranced about in the snow. Reindeer just LOVE

snow, you know. Santa took some food out of his sleigh

and held it out to the reindeer. It stopped prancing and

shyly approached.
```

Let's take the layout shown at the top of the opposite page in miniature and size it for the printer. We pick 12 pt. Century Expanded for our type. By consulting the characters-per-pica chart we find that there are 2.2 characters of this type in 1 pica. By actual measurement on our layout, the length of the lines (measure) is 18 picas. So there are 40 characters (approx.) of this type in 18 picas (2.2 × 18 = 39.6 or 40 characters). Count over 40 characters (including word spaces and punctuation marks) on the manuscript and mark it. Draw a perpendicular line through this mark as shown above. There are 4 full lines of text to the left of this line. Count the characters to the right of the vertical line, add the characters of the last 2 words, and divide the total by 40. This gives us 3 lines, and added to the 4 we have a total of 7 lines. We feel we need 2 pts. of leading between the lines. You can now calculate the total depth the type will be. If this depth checks with your layout, spec the manuscript and order the type. Proofread the proofs when they come back and if they are perfect, paste them in position on your mechanical.

The Reproduction Proof

Then suddenly, out of the storm there appeared…a reindeer! It leaped and pranced about in the snow. Reindeer just LOVE snow, you know. Santa took some food out of his sleigh and held it out to the reindeer. It stopped prancing and shyly approached.

How to "spec" (specify) type for the printer

① If you have more than 1 page, number all the pages of your typed manuscript.

② Be sure the copy you give to the printer is letter-perfect — no mistakes.

③ Type all the copy, double spaced, no wider than 5½" and centered on an 8½" x 11" sheet. Use the margins for marking up the copy.

④ Write the date you want the proofs, and how many and what kind you want (reproduction, Kleenstik, correction galleys, or any others) at the top of the first page of your manuscript.

⑤ If you have any question about anything call and ask the printer who is setting your job.

⑥ Always send a sketch of your type arrangements, from your layout, with your specs to the printer.

⑦ Mark any copy on the manuscript that you do not want set "delete" (possibly hand-lettering or logotypes, for example).

⑧ Always give the complete names of the typeface styles. (Get them from a type specimen book.)

⑨ Before you send it out, always check your job.

⑩ Write clear, legible instructions.

⑪ Write "The end" on the last page of the manuscript when there is more than one page.

⑫ Sign every sheet (at the bottom) and give your company's name and telephone number.

Shown below are some accepted abbreviations and symbols used in marking your manuscript. See how they are used in the example on the next page.

u & l.c.	upper and lowercase	/	after a word this indicates where you want the line to end
$\frac{12}{14}$	12 pt. type, 2 pt. leading	≡	under a letter or word means caps
pt.	abbreviation for point	=	under a letter or word, small caps
#	symbol for space	—	under a word means italic

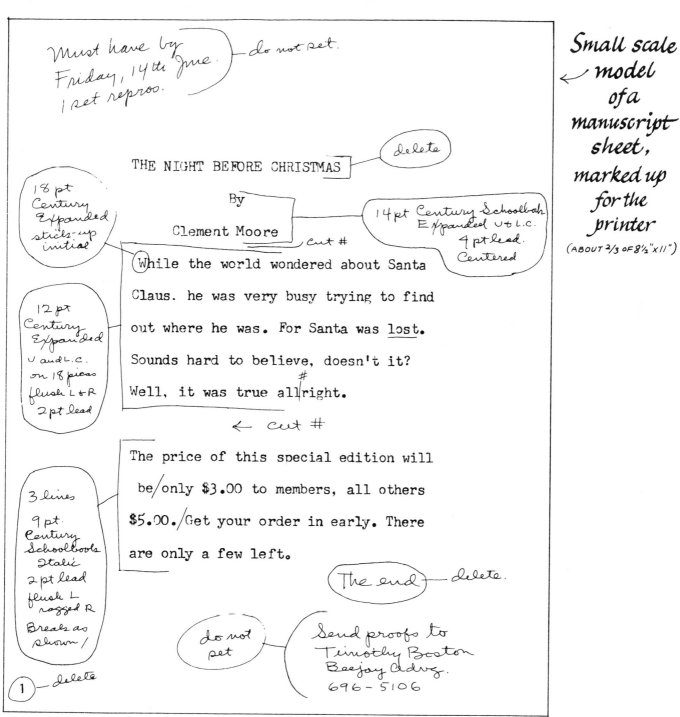

Must have by Friday, 14th June. — do not set. I set repros.

Small scale model of a manuscript sheet, marked up for the printer (ABOUT 2/3 OF 8½"×11")

THE NIGHT BEFORE CHRISTMAS — delete

18 pt Century Expanded stick-up initial

By

Clement Moore — cut #

14 pt Century Schoolbook Expanded U & L.C. 4 pt lead. Centered

While the world wondered about Santa
Claus. he was very busy trying to find
out where he was. For Santa was lost.
Sounds hard to believe, doesn't it?
Well, it was true all#right.

12 pt Century Expanded U and L.C. on 18 picas flush L & R 2 pt lead

← cut #

The price of this special edition will
be/only $3.00 to members, all others
$5.00./Get your order in early. There
are only a few left.

3 lines 9 pt. Century Schoolbook Italic 2 pt lead flush L ragged R Breaks as shown /

The end — delete.

do not set

Send proofs to Timothy Boston Beejay Advg. 696-5106

① — delete

Do not be too wordy. However, if some unusal effect is desired, describe it as simply and clearly as you can. If it is too complicated, call the printer, or have him call you when he gets your specs.

How to align vertically the right-hand margin of text with a typewriter

If you type the same copy twice, you can align the right-hand margin of typewritten matter by following the suggestions below. Done in this manner, mimeographed company newspapers or typed advertisements sent in the mail will have a more professional look.

The first Six Months Award for perfect//
time and attendance records under the///
STAR Program will be made later this////
month. The 30 Plant employees still////
eligible represent 13 different depart-/
ments in the manufacturing and distri-//
bution areas.

Leading are Machine Finishing and Die///
Cut with five candidates each and///////
Machine Shop with seven. Die Cut had a/
sixth until John Doe was promoted to////
Supervisor and therefore became/////////
ineligible for the award. Other de-////
partments with employees in the running/
include Platform, Warehouse, Everyday///
Picking, Ribbon Converting, Seasonal////
Packaging, Everyday Packaging, Machine//
Fold, Stamping, Trim and Gift Dressing./

At the June 17 STAR Awards presentation/
in the Cafeteria, honors went to all////

←——— *PENCIL LINES* ———→

The first Six Months Award for perfect
time and attendance records under the
STAR Program will be made later this
month. The 30 Plant Employees still
eligible represent 13 different depart-
ments in the manufacturing and distri-
bution areas.

Leading are Machine Finishing and Die
Cut with five candidates each   and
Machine Shop with seven. Die cut had a
sixth until John Doe was promoted to
Supervisor and   therefore   became
ineligible for the award. Other de-
partments with employees in the running
include Platform, Warehouse,   Everyday
Picking, Ribbon Converting,   Seasonal
Packaging, Everyday Packaging, Machine
Fold, Stamping, Trim and Gift Dressing.

At the June 17 STAR Awards   presentation
in   the Cafeteria, honors went   to all

Draw the limits of your margins with pencil and type your material within these limits. As you near the right-hand pencil line, you must decide if you have space for the next word. If you do not, fill the line with slashes to the pencil line.

When you retype the material, allow extra spaces between words until the number of slash marks are used up. When you are finished, all of the lines of your copy should look like the typewritten copy above, with the right-hand margin perfectly aligned vertically.

Having fun with words

A word or words in a caption or logotype or trademark may suggest a treatment which emphasizes the meaning of the word. The examples below show how amusing it can be to use type this way.

ceNsOred

$ue

snuggle

CHAPEL

ejec t

MONA LISA

S K
 I
  N
   G

c( )wboy

Question

MARRIAGE

PERI.D

grow

MISTAKE

HDE

CARTOON

in c o m e
TAX

about
face

PINC

para=el

DIVO RCE

TR

L NELY

PRIS N

ZY
C

ABS NT

STROLL

ANGRRRY

T NNEL

ARE YOU AFRAID?

How to mark a point without measuring

Suppose you have a type proof that you want to be sure fits a certain area on an already partly designed layout. You want to check certain points of the type with similar points on your layout.

   Hold the proof in the position you want over the layout. Hold a pencil or some other pointer with the other hand, the butt of the hand resting firmly on the drawing board and the pointer touching the type's margin. Pull the proof away but do not move the marker. Your mark is now established on the layout.

The type proof

The same method can be used for marking points in other situations.

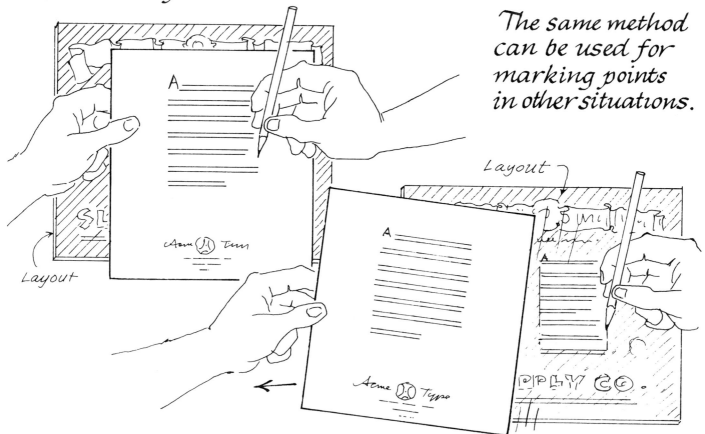

Layout

Layout

How to achieve order in a design

Here are only a few ways that the graphic designer can achieve order in his layouts.

A CAT NAMED PI
Once upon a time, in a lone little village at

Keep the caption and text style the same. You achieve unity of type most effectively in this way.

Coach	FERD SONDERN
Mr. Simsi	GEORGE PORTER
Siss	LILI GAYDOS
Chairman	STEPHANIE HARRIS
Sammy	HAL GREER

Common alignments give unity to an arrangement.

The left edge of the type "follows" the illustration's irregular edge.

Center all elements for a symmetric balance. Lines arranged in this manner have great unity.

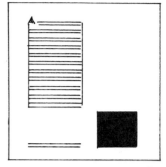

In this example of asymmetric balance, the large gray area at the top left balances the small black element on the lower right.

The 2 most common methods to have type set for a neat and unified look are shown below.

Flush left and right type lines.

Flush left type lines with ragged right. Flush right and ragged left is not used often.

Lettering
How to sketch classic roman capital letters

The <u>set</u> of a letter is the relationship of its width to its height. The beauty of lettering depends, therefore, on the artist's understanding of the sets of all letters according to classic roman tradition, accepted through the ages as the ideal of beautiful letter form. The basic sets of those classic forms are shown here. Anyone applying this information will be well on his or her way to accomplishing good lettering. Other factors of lettering are important, but the set is the most important one.

Square set
Limits fall within a square.

Narrow set
Width is less than a square.

Wide set
Width is more than a square.

"M" is another wide-set letter

The 2 thin letters

Rest of square-set letters

Rest of narrow-set letters

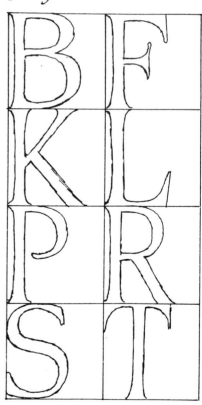

These sets are to be followed whether the letter is sans serif, speedball, square serif, or any other type of letter.

How to identify parts of letters correctly

Anyone concerned with designing, not just letterers, should be able to identify and name the parts of letters correctly. Here is the correct terminology for roman letter forms.

Terms refer to those parts of letters encircled when circles or ovals are shown.

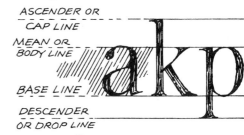

Guide lines

SHADED PART REFERS TO THE WAIST OR BODY OF THE LETTER

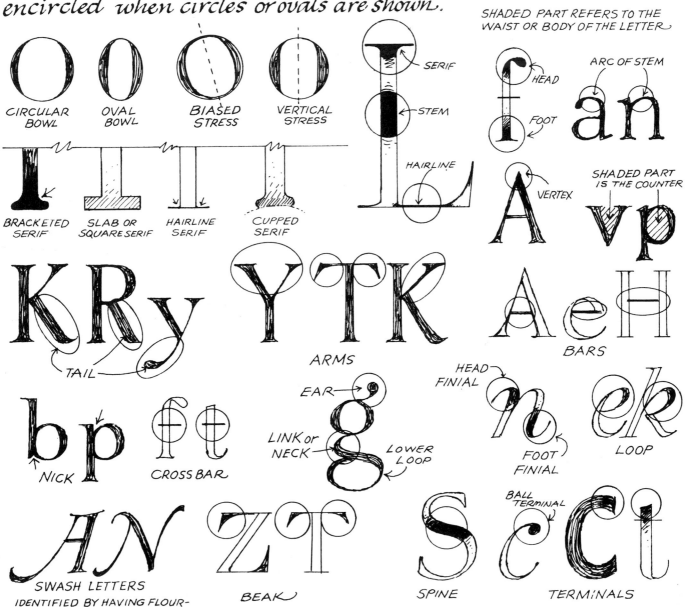

CIRCULAR BOWL   OVAL BOWL   BIASED STRESS   VERTICAL STRESS

SERIF   STEM   HAIRLINE

HEAD   ARC OF STEM   FOOT

BRACKETED SERIF   SLAB OR SQUARE SERIF   HAIRLINE SERIF   CUPPED SERIF

VERTEX   SHADED PART IS THE COUNTER

TAIL   ARMS   BARS

EAR   HEAD FINIAL

NICK   CROSS BAR   LINK or NECK   LOWER LOOP   FOOT FINIAL   LOOP

BALL TERMINAL

SWASH LETTERS
IDENTIFIED BY HAVING FLOURISHED TAILS AND TERMINALS

BEAK   SPINE   TERMINALS

49

How to identify the major styles of lettering

Old Style Roman

The height of the letter is 9 to 11 times the thickness of the stem (the heavy stroke). Hairline stroke (the thin stroke) is about ½ the size of thick stroke. Serifs are heavy, rounded and cupped. The style has a hand-drawn look.

Curved letters have vertical stress

Modern Roman

The set of this letter is the same as with the old style. There is great contrast between the stem and the hairline strokes. Serifs are hairline, with no fillets. It looks mechanically drawn.

A

Sans (without) Serif

The set is the same as o.s.* It looks like the same thickness of stroking throughout. There are no serifs. When the set changes from classic roman, the style is called grotesk, gothic or a number of other styles, all of which have no serifs. * old style roman

About

Formal Script

This form is slanted, joined, and looks written, although it is carefully designed. It is sometimes called Spencerian after Charles Spencer, an early writing master.

Friends

Informal Script

This is a casual, vertical written form – with no definite requirements other than that it can be read.

Manch

Calligraphy

The slanted, written formal letter is done with a flat-edged tool (chisel-edged pencil, brush, or pen.)

Medí

Black Text

This truly Gothic lettering looks medieval. It is heavy, vertical and condensed.

A

Square Serif

This letter has square or slab serifs and a roman set. It is mechanical-looking.

bint

Italic

Non-joining, slanted formal letters are carefully designed and named after "Italy," where they originated.

Decorative

Here obviously ornamented, the letters can be a basic form with ornaments and shading.

These remarks are very general. More study of the subject would be required to become an accomplished letterer.

How to use a chisel-edged tool to form letters

The "mystery" of how to make letters thick and thin, and where, is un-locked if the artist understands that the chisel-edged tool, held at one angle to a horizontal line, forms the thick and thin lines in letters.

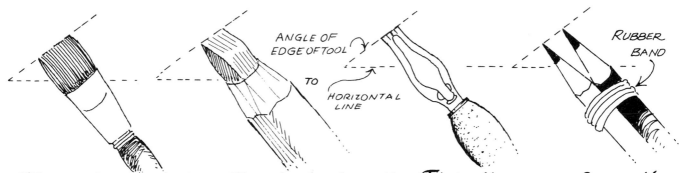

Flat-edged brush   **Chisel-edged pencil**   **Flat-nib pen**   **2 pencils**

The dotted lines above shows the consistent angle to be maintained. The tool is held comfortably in any easy manner. All the tools shown can be used like a chisel-edged tool.

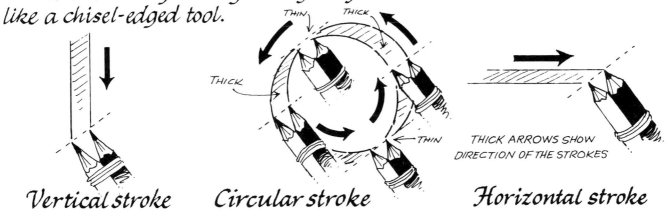

Vertical stroke   **Circular stroke**   **Horizontal stroke**

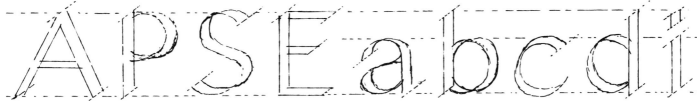

Following simple letter forms, and holding the tool's edge at the same angle as demonstrated above, practice drawing the letters. Forms can be "finished off" later with a single pointed pencil or other tool. Serifs, if wanted, can be added in the same way.

How to sketch a good letter "S"

Of the 26 letters in the alphabet, "S" is one of the most difficult ones to draw. A few simple suggestions will result in a well-drawn letter that should be acceptable and will have the benefit of being personally created.

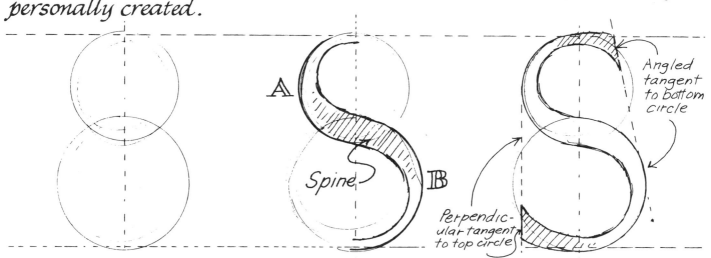

Between 2 guide lines and centered on a perpendicular line, freely sketch 2 slightly overlapping circles. The top circle should be slightly smaller than the bottom circle. Next draw the spine and emphasize the circular parts at A and B. Then form the terminal endings as shown. The terminal at the top right is slanted on a line tangent to the bottom at B; at the bottom left it is perpendicular. All of the curves should flow into each other—without bumps. The serifs can be designed in a variety of ways. As you try other possibilities like the S's shown below, remember that at A and B the form must always be circular, or parts of regular ovals.

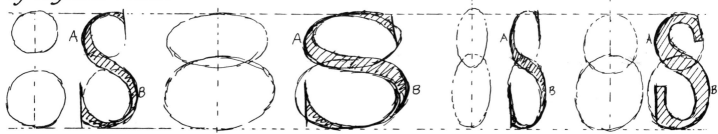

How to make letters for an effective wall sign

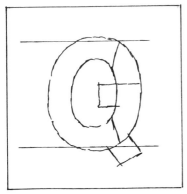

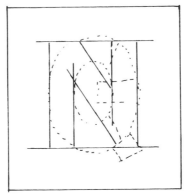

First sketch a basic letter, O, on tracing paper. Use this same letter and sketch the others, C, G, and Q, that are based on the O.

With the first sketch under a new piece of tracing paper, draw the rest of the letters needed for the job.

With a stylus, or a hard pencil, trace the letters on a foil cardboard and then cut them out with a small stencil knife and scissors.

The letters can then be spaced and glued to the wall. Start in the center of your message and work toward either end. The sample below is a copy of a sign that was actually used. The letters, which were 15" high, were pasted onto a white tile wall. The rubber cement which was used was easily cleaned off the wall later.

Numerals

Some information about arabic and roman numerals

Arabic number	Roman equivalent
1	I
2	II
4	IV
5	V
6	VI
7	VII
9	IX
10	X
11	XI
20	XX
30	XXX
40	XL
41	XLI
49	IL
50	L
60	LX
90	XC
100	C
101	CI
150	CL
200	CC
400	CD
500	D
600	DC
900	CM
1000	M
1976	MCMLXXVI
2000	MM
5000	$\overline{V}$
10,000	$\overline{X}$
100,000	$\overline{C}$
1,000,000	$\overline{M}$

Nonaligning Numerals
(Old Style)

1 2 3 4 5 6 7 8 9 0

The above line consists of numbers that are "up-and-down", that is, nonaligning; they are the numbers we got from the arabs or moors in Spain. Only "1" and "0" are within the guide lines. The even numbers are above the guide lines while the odd numbers fall below the base line.

Aligning Numerals
(Modern)

1 2 3 4 5 6 7 8 9 0

The above line of numbers is called aligning numerals because all the numbers fit within the 2 guide lines. With the exception of the number "1", they are the same width — at least they appear to be. Because of this and because they align, they are conveniently used in columns and in tabular information.

The bar above the letters is a part of the symbol.

54

Drawing and Painting
How to keep watercolors moist

Expensive watercolors, designers' colors, tempera, or other water-based paint can be kept moist and workable indefinitely if you use the following suggestion. This will also save you money because you will not waste paint.

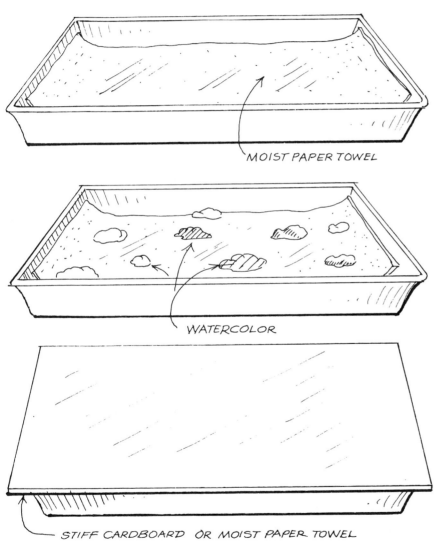

MOIST PAPER TOWEL

WATERCOLOR

STIFF CARDBOARD OR MOIST PAPER TOWEL

Line the bottom of a shallow cookie pan, or similar waterproof container, with a paper towel — the kind that is found in wall dispensers.

Moisten the towel but do not saturate it with water. The towel can be kept damp with periodic applications of small amounts of water. Squeeze paint onto the damp towel as you need it. Arrange the colors as you would on any palette, allowing enough space between the colors for intermixing other colors.

Place a damp towel or a heavy flat oversize card over the top of the cookie tin for the weekend. Your paint should be moist and ready for use when you get back.

How to paint a light-colored object against a dark background when painting a transparent watercolor

Suppose you want to paint a transparent watercolor painting with a light yellow ocher tree against a dark background as in the picture at left. Usually the artist paints around the tree with the dark background color. The method described here is much better because you get sharper definition and can paint over the tree quickly with the background color.

← First sketch out the composition and draw in the tree with a yellow wax crayon.

Proceed to paint the watercolor until it is finished, except for the tree. When the background color is dry, remove the crayon tree with a wad of cotton and rubber cement thinner. You will find that it can be completely removed, allowing you then to paint in the yellow ocher tree in watercolor.

Foreground grasses, weeds, and light-colored flowers with dark green grass background can also be done in the same manner.

How to soften or modify marker-pen drawings

Turpentine and rubber cement thinner are solvents for most waterproof marker pens. Water is a solvent for the water-soluble markers.

Interesting effects can be obtained by using swabs, Q-tips, rags, and the proper solvent for softening edges and other parts of a drawing already made with marker pens.

Experiment — and see for yourself.

Turpentine and thinner will clean marker marks and smudges on acetate and most hard nonabsorbent surfaces.

Simple ways to draw on the side of a container

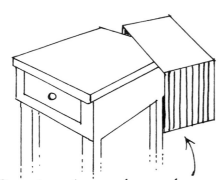

Box is placed on the corner of a table. The right hand rests on the table top. The left hand holds the box against the table corner.

Use a large or small table, depending on what works best.

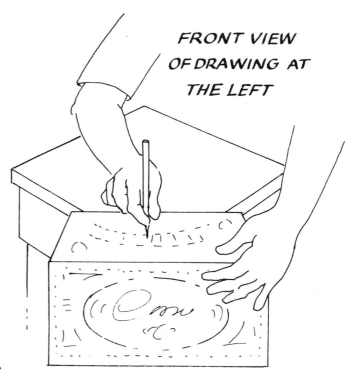

FRONT VIEW OF DRAWING AT THE LEFT

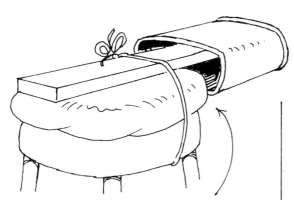

A long flat stick is tied to a chair top and used as an arm rest. Container is placed over the stick and held while being worked on.

The corner of a large flat book on top of a round chair seat holds the box. This is the same principle that is shown in the illustration above

Pile books around a square or round box. A small flat book is used as an arm or hand rest.

Drawing Lines and Edges

How to use a straight edge for drawing lines

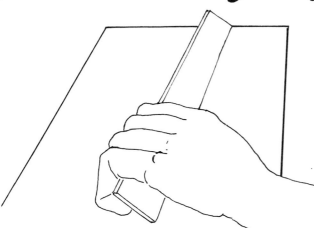

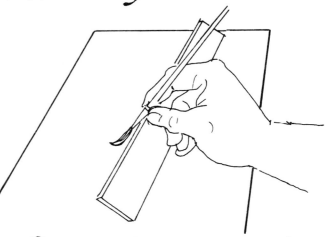

Position of the left hand holding the ruler. The finger-tips are on the drawing surface.

Position of the right hand holding the brush against the ruler.

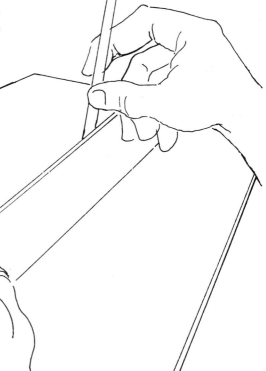

A pen, brush, or other tool can be used expediently against a ruler for drawing straight lines as shown.

The ruler is held rigidly on the drawing surface by the left hand.

The brush is held against the edge of the ruler and drawn from left to right.

Practice this and it will soon be an easy operation.

Practice spread, dotted, and other lines.

How to divide any line into equal parts without a ruler

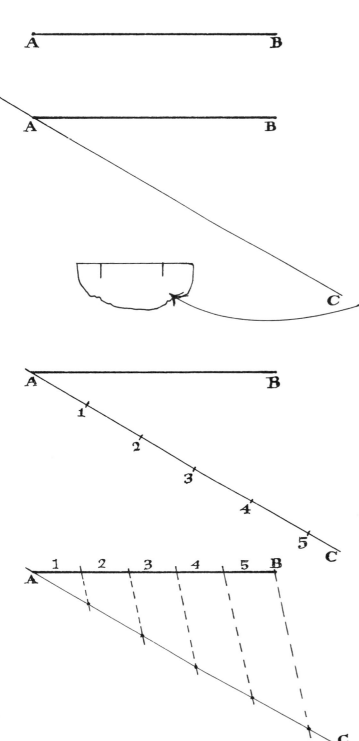

Let the line which we wish to divide into five equal parts be AB.

Construct a line through A to any distance. This line is marked AC and is at any angle to AB.

On a straight-edge piece of paper mark any distance with two marks. This is your marking piece.

Using this marking piece, measure off the desired number of divisions (e.g., 5 here). You do not have to meet C — AC is just an arbitrary line.

Turn the paper so that the 5th mark and B line up on your T square. As you draw parallel lines for all the marks, you divide AB into 5 equal parts (where the lines cross).

How to draw expedient parallel lines

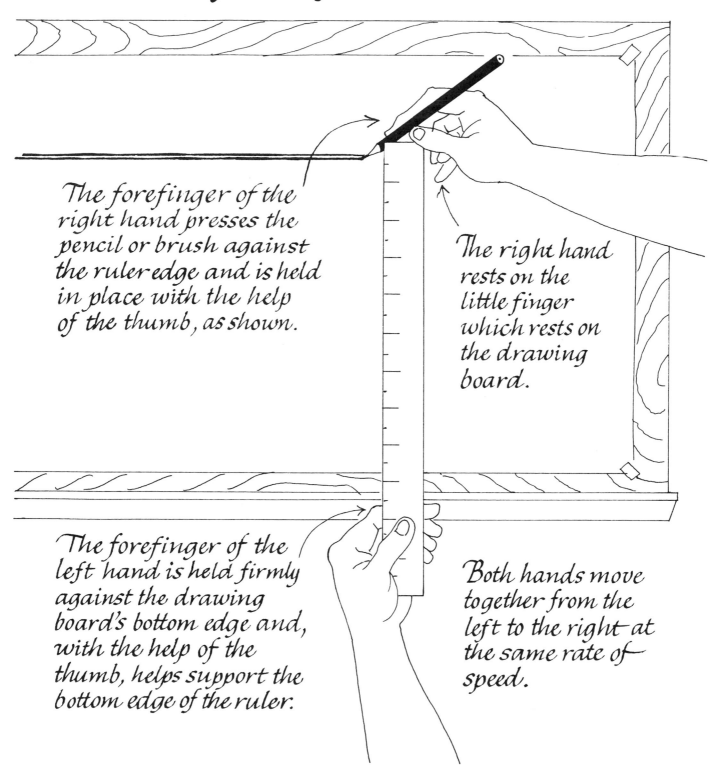

The forefinger of the right hand presses the pencil or brush against the ruler edge and is held in place with the help of the thumb, as shown.

The right hand rests on the little finger which rests on the drawing board.

The forefinger of the left hand is held firmly against the drawing board's bottom edge and, with the help of the thumb, helps support the bottom edge of the ruler.

Both hands move together from the left to the right at the same rate of speed.

Easy ways to get straight edges on color blocks and lettering

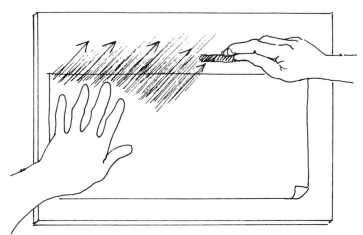

Suppose you wanted to indicate a color area with a straight edge on a layout. Hold a straight-edged paper in the place where you want the straight edge to be. Hold the paper firmly so it does not slip. With a sweeping motion of your ⌐ pencil, pastel, or other tool, and from bottom to top only, swish in strokes across the straight edge, as in the drawing at the left above. When you are finished, remove the paper. You should have an effect similar to the drawing above.

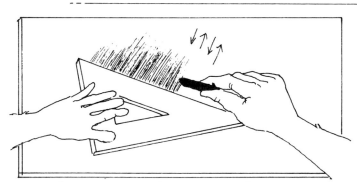

The straight edge of a triangle can be used for drawing straight edges. Hold it firmly where you want the straight edge and bring your tool up to the edge of the triangle, not across the edge.

The straight edge of a piece of paper can be used to align the bottoms of letters in display headlines. When the paper is removed after drawing the letters, the letters will be perfected aligned.

Forming Circles, Ovals, and Spirals
How to draw a circle with no visible center mark

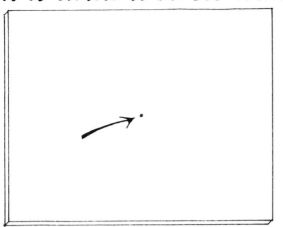

① With a pencil, determine exactly where the center of the circle will be on the art.

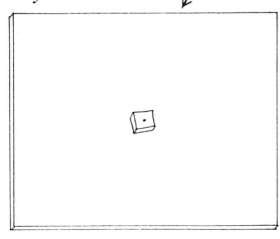

② Cut a small square out of illustration board and rubber cement it over the center of the circle. ⤵

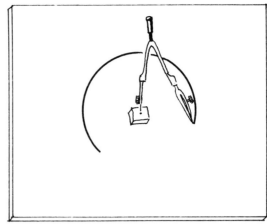

③ Draw a circle with an ink or pencil compass.

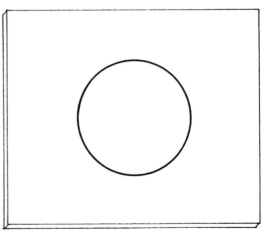

④ After you remove the center card and clean away the rubber cement, you are left with a circle that has no visible center mark.

Apply this method in other instances where pinprick holes on the art are to be avoided.

How to draw a circle through any three points not on a straight line

B

A

C

①

Suppose you have 3 points not on a straight line and want to draw a circle through them.

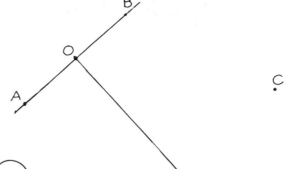

②

First draw a line between A and B; divide it in half (at O). At O, construct a perpendicular line.

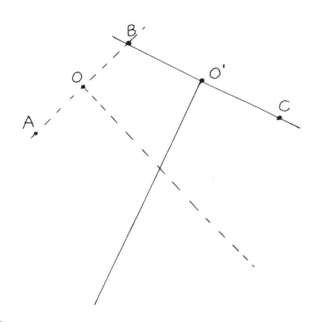

③

Then draw a line between B and C, divide it in half (at O'), and construct another perpendicular line.

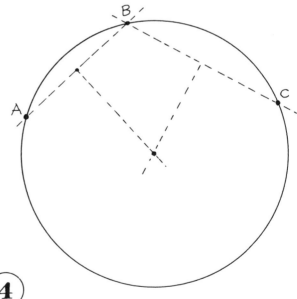

④

Where the perpendicular lines intersect is the center for the circle.

How to cut a paper circle of any size

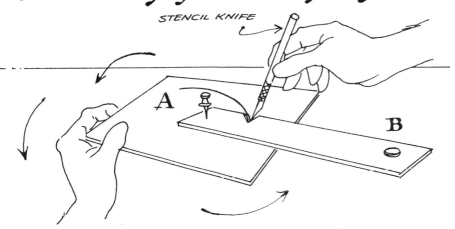

STENCIL KNIFE

On the paper, A, stick a pushpin firmly through the proposed center of the circle. From this center to the notch cut in the long card is the radius of the circle to be cut. The long strip is a thin card with a pushpin, thumbtack, or other fastener firmly stabilizing the card at B. You cut a circle by rotating the paper around the notch, which holds the stencil knife in position.

How to draw a large circle or arc

A long string or cord can be used for drawing extremely large circles or arcs. Or it may be more convenient for you to use a long strip of cardboard or a long strip of wood. The center of the circle is at A and the strip is secured there. Punch a small hole at the other end, B, to allow for the insertion of a pencil point or the tip of a technical pen that will make the arc line.

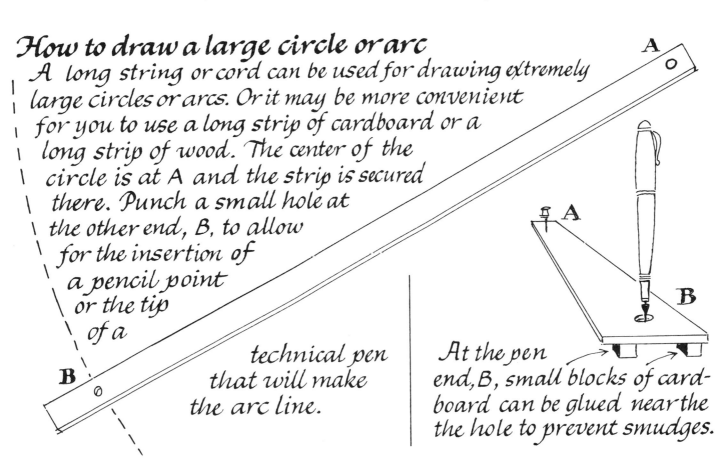

At the pen end, B, small blocks of cardboard can be glued near the the hole to prevent smudges.

How to draw a circle with a brush and compass

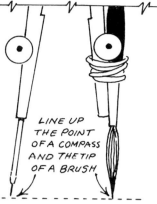

LINE UP THE POINT OF A COMPASS AND THE TIP OF A BRUSH

First remove the lead from the compass and extend the center point out as far as you can to make room for the brush's hair to clear the compass when the brush is attached.

The brush is fastened to the lead leg of the compass with a rubber band, tape, or string. Spread the compass to the desired radius and dip the brush into the ink or paint.

Circles can be drawn freely, quickly, or very carefully this way. Try spread lines and other kinds of lines. Try a dry-brush effect. Experiment with textures of papers. Have fun.

How to sketch a free-hand oval

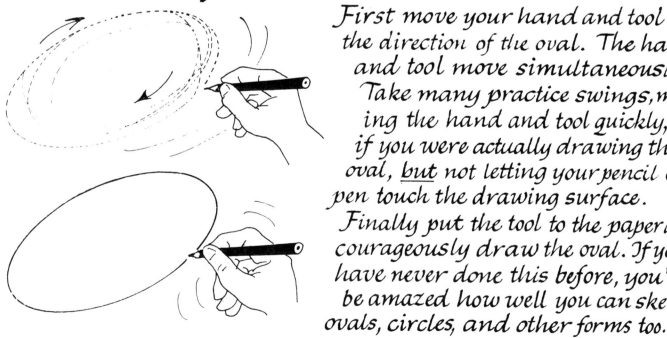

First move your hand and tool in the direction of the oval. The hand and tool move simultaneously.

Take many practice swings, moving the hand and tool quickly, as if you were actually drawing the oval, but not letting your pencil or pen touch the drawing surface.

Finally put the tool to the paper and courageously draw the oval. If you have never done this before, you'll be amazed how well you can sketch ovals, circles, and other forms too.

How to draw a round corner

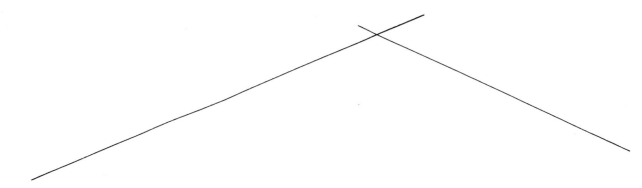

Suppose that you had 2 intersecting lines that form a pointed corner but you want a round corner instead.

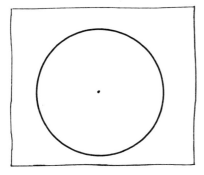

First obtain the curve by drawing a circle of any size you want on a separate piece of paper.

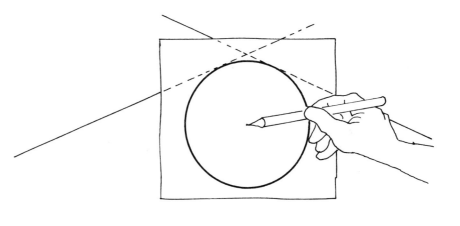

An arc of this circle will become the round corner. Move the paper around until the circle is tangent to the 2 intersecting lines. Mark the center of the circle, remove the paper and draw the arc. You now have a round corner.

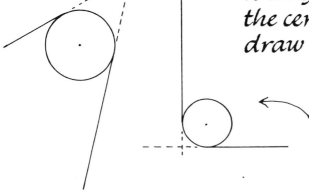

This method can be used for making round corners on any intersecting lines regardless of the angle they make.

How to draw an oval of any size

Suppose you wish to draw an oval 2⅛" long (major axis) and 1⅝" high (minor axis).

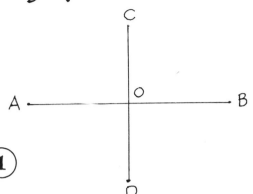

① Draw the major axis AB and the minor axis CD. The axes will be perpendicular to and bisecting each other at O.

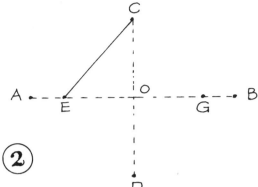

② Find E and G on the major axis. CE and CG are equal to ½ of the major axis (AO or OB).

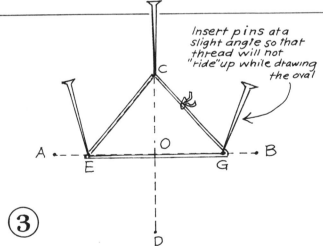

Insert pins at a slight angle so that thread will not "ride" up while drawing the oval

③ Insert pins at 3 points: C, E, and G. Loop a thin strong thread around the bottom of the pins tautly and tie a knot. Then, remove the pin at C.

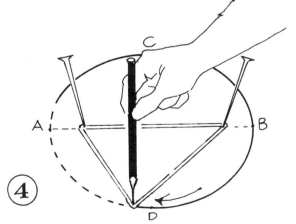

④ When you insert a tool, pencil, or pen into the loop and radiate it around the pins, as shown above, you will draw an oval which passes through points A, B, C, and D.

How to draw a spiral with a pencil or pen

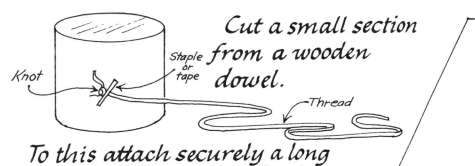

Cut a small section from a wooden dowel.

To this attach securely a long strong thread. Glue the dowel to illustration board or whatever surface you want to draw the spiral on.

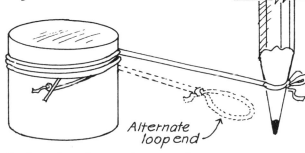

Attach the thread to a pencil end and wrap it around the dowel. As you unwind the string, the pencil will form a spiral. Use different size dowels for spirals of varied sizes. The finished spiral can be photostatted larger or smaller if desired.

A technical pen can be used in the same manner for an _inked_ spiral. When using this pen, wrap a small piece of tape around the nib near the tip. This prevents the end of the thread from touching the inked line.

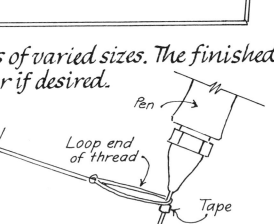

How to "draw" spirals quickly

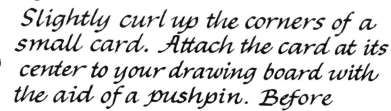

Slightly curl up the corners of a small card. Attach the card at its center to your drawing board with the aid of a pushpin. Before attaching, rotate the pin around the hole so that the hole is slightly larger than the shank of the push-pin. Hold the brush's tip, with paint, near the card's center. Spin the card with your other hand and immediately apply the brush to the card near the center, and move to the outside as the card spins.

Experiment with different kinds of lines and colors.

How to use a turntable to draw a spiral

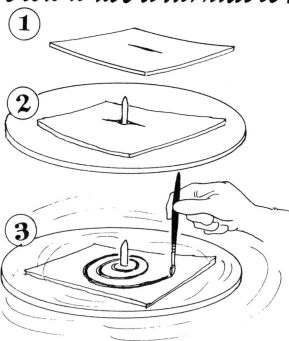

A record player can be used to draw many kinds of free spirals. Take a stiff card and cut a slit as shown in ①. Push the card through the spindle of the turntable ②, ink a brush, turn the player on and have fun ③. Pressure on the brush now and then will create interesting spread line effects.

After drawing one spiral, and while the turntable is still moving, try another color over the one you just completed. Try other effects, like moving the brush to the outside more slowly.

Drawing a Polygon
How to draw a regular polygon with any number of sides

Assume you want to draw a pentagon and a 5-point star...

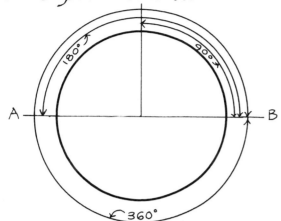

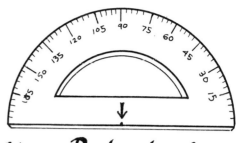

Use a **Protractor** for measuring angles.

On a circle, draw line AB. After dividing 360° (total number of degrees in a circle) by 5 (the desired division) and getting 72°, use the protractor to measure these continuous 72° angles and you will get points A, B, C, D, and E (see below). These points are now joined to form either a pentagon or a 5-pointed star. If you want a six-sided figure, divide 360° by 6 (60°) and proceed as you did with the 5-pointed polygon. If you want a 10-sided figure, divide 360° by 10 (36°), and so on. By trial and error, you must add a little or subtract a little with figures that are not easily divided into 360°.

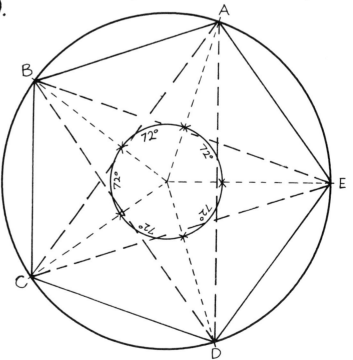

Brushes and Pens

How to make a carrier for brushes and pens

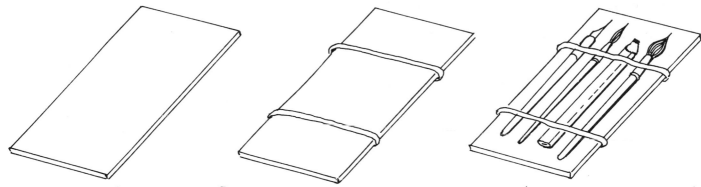

Cut a stiff card any convenient size, such as pocket size.

Stretch two rubber bands around the card – one at the top, one at the bottom –

and insert the brushes and pens under the rubber bands for carrying.

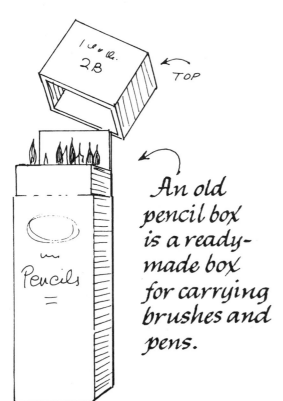

An old pencil box is a ready-made box for carrying brushes and pens.

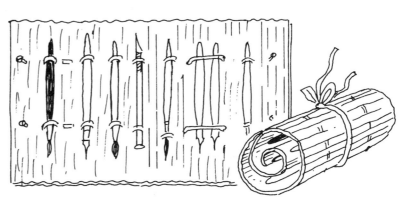

An old bamboo mat or an old place mat with brushes and pens neatly laid inside can be rolled and tied. A thread or rubber band can be laced in and out of the top and bottom of the mat to hold everything in place.

Tips on brushes

Mark one good brush (with white tape, e.g.) for use with white paint <u>only</u>. You will always have clean white strokes if you do this. <u>Never</u> use this brush with <u>any</u> color in it.

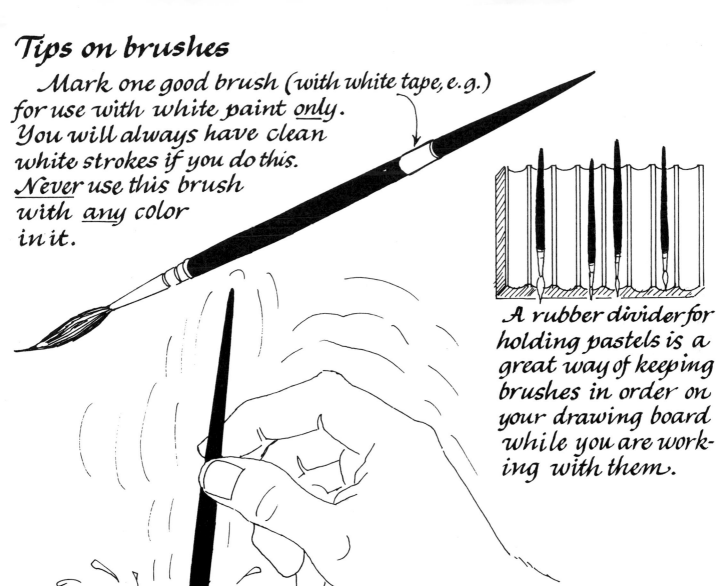

A rubber divider for holding pastels is a great way of keeping brushes in order on your drawing board while you are working with them.

Never put down a brush that has color or ink in it without first washing it out in a water jar. Keep the brush soft and clean until you can really wash it out later. The brush will be much harder to clean if you let paint or ink dry in the hair.

How to reshape an old turned brush

If you have an old neglected brush that you think could still be usable, even though it is split and turned, immerse it into a water-soluble glue or mucilage (5 and 10¢ store items).

Then work the hairs between your fingers and shape them. Continue this action until the brush is almost dry. The brush can then be hung and left suspended for a few days to dry. Or you can punch the brush's handle through a thin card and stand it in an empty glass or cup to dry. After a few days, wash the brush. By then it should have its normal manufactured shape back. If not, throw it away.

How to help maintain technical pens

The best way to keep a technical pen in good working order is to follow the instructions that come with the pen when you buy it. If, for some reason, you have neglected to do so and you find that your pen needs cleaning, these instructions will help.

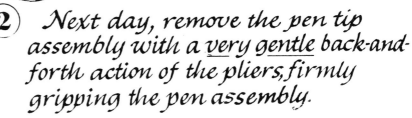

TWIST LEFT AND RIGHT GENTLY

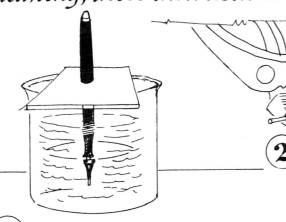

① Suspend the pen in warm detergent water or recommended ink solvent. Leave it suspended overnight.

② Next day, remove the pen tip assembly with a _very gentle_ back-and-forth action of the pliers, firmly gripping the pen assembly.

STOP

PLUNGER

PEN POINT

③ Separate the elements of the point and _carefully_ clean them.

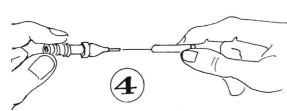

④ _Carefully_ use the plunger in reverse, as you would thread a needle, to clean the pen point. _Do not bend the plunger wire._

⑤ Fill the tip with warm water and carefully force a Q-tip into the open end of the point. Water should jet out when the point is clean. Dry all the parts and reassemble the pen.

How to use poster and tempera color in a ruling pen

Poster and tempera watercolor can be thinned with water and put into a ruling pen with the aid of a brush.

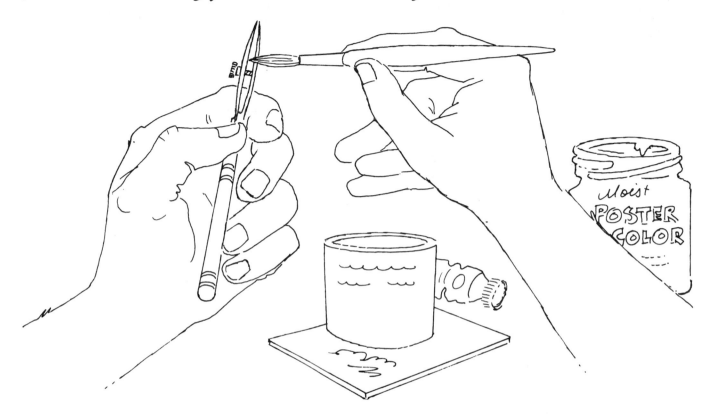

The ruling pen can then be used against a T square, triangle, and any other formed template you may design. From time to time, squeeze the blades of the ruling pen together and run the brush through the the blades to keep the color moist and wet enough to flow onto your drawing. While lines drawn in this manner may be a lighter value than the color you fill in later between the lines, the value change will be insignificant.

Other materials, such as oil paint, silk screen color, and acrylics can be inserted in a ruling pen and used in the same manner but you must work fast AND clean the pen thoroughly after you have used it.

How spraying minimizes marker bleeding and creeping

If you use marker felt-nib pens on porous or semiporous paper or cards for signs, charts, or other purposes, spray your working area first with fixative. This minimizes bleeding and creeping of forms into each other, especially if the lines are close together as in A to the left. Some bleeding and creeping may occur if you just spray with workable fixative first. For maximum effectiveness spray your working area generously with acrylic spray coating and when the area is dry, proceed with your work. The images you draw will now be clear-cut as in B compared to A.

Always test on scrap paper first.

How to make a fussy ball-point pen work

You can do something about a ball point pen not working, providing it has ink in it. Touch the tip of the pen to something hot (like a cigarette tip or a flame), and it will work. Also, a new tip sometimes has a coating on it which must be removed before the pen will work properly.

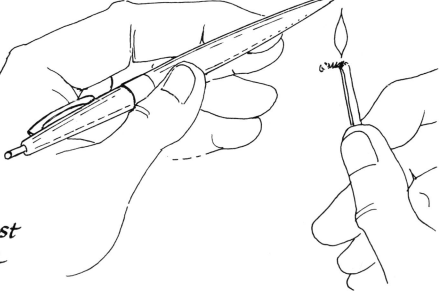

How to "mark time" on ink bottles

All artists who work with ink know how frustrating it is to pick up and use a bottle of old ink just as they are about to ink in a drawing.

To avoid this, mark your bottles with the date on which you receive them. You can write the date on a small piece of white tape and adhere it to the side of the bottle or container.

How to make a home-made humidor for technical pens

Take an old clean jar with a screw-on top. On the inside of the jar top, glue a small sponge, using waterproof glue. (Be sure that the jar size will accommodate technical pens.)

Keep the sponge wet (not dripping) and close the jar with the technical pens that you use, with ink in them, inside. They will stay workable as long as the sponge is damp and the top is tightly screwed on. This is a great way to store pens for weekends. Be sure that the tip ends of the pens are up.

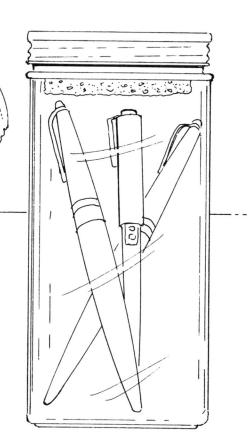

Pencils
How to make selecting the right pencil easier:

If you use many grades of lead in mechanical pencils, it is a good idea to use one pencil for each grade of lead and mark the grade with a white tape on all sides of the pencil shaft, as shown. You will then never have difficulty picking up the right pencil grade.

Another method is to mark the sides of the pencil with black or white paint and apply varnish spray to the mark.

How to speed up a pencil rendering

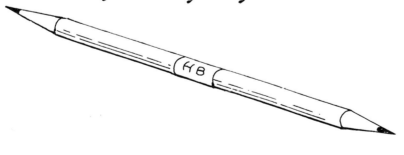

If you are using a wood-clenched pencil and are in a hurry to complete an assignment sharpen both ends of the pencil. This will save time; just switch around to the other end when one end becomes blunt. Mark the grade of the lead on a tape and attach to the center of the pencil. If you like, one end of the pencil can have a chisel edge, the other a point.

Information about pencils

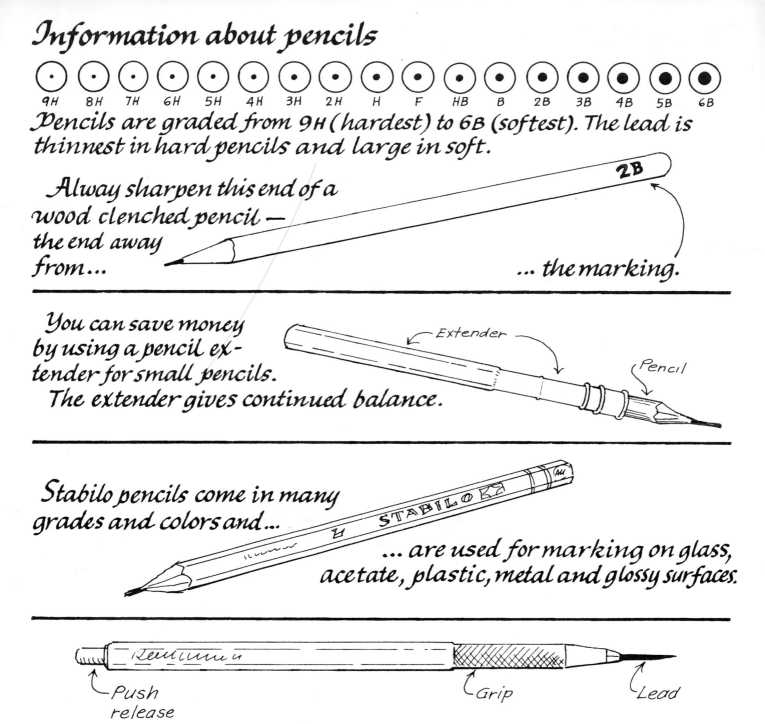

| 9H | 8H | 7H | 6H | 5H | 4H | 3H | 2H | H | F | HB | B | 2B | 3B | 4B | 5B | 6B |

Pencils are graded from 9H (hardest) to 6B (softest). The lead is thinnest in hard pencils and large in soft.

Alway sharpen this end of a wood clenched pencil — the end away from...

... the marking.

2B

You can save money by using a pencil extender for small pencils.
The extender gives continued balance.

Extender

Pencil

Stabilo pencils come in many grades and colors and...

... are used for marking on glass, acetate, plastic, metal and glossy surfaces.

STABILO

Push release

Grip

Lead

Mechanical pencils are most economical. When needed, leads are easily replaced and can be purchased in all grades which are interchangeable in the same pencil.

Ways to Work with Other Materials and Tools
5 ways to flatten a curled print

A curled print is carefully uncurled in the direction opposite the curl on a cardboard tube, fastened at the ends with tape, and left for a few days.

①

② *If the print is nonglossy the back of the print can be worked back and forth against a smooth corner.*

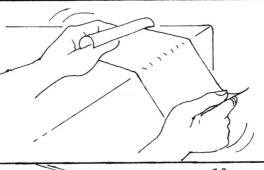

③ 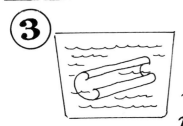 First soak the print, if it is unretouched, in water for 5 or 10 minutes. Then hang the wet print on a clothesline and weight it at the bottom.

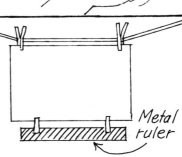

Metal ruler

④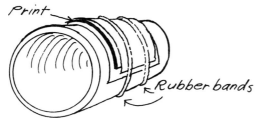

Print

Rubber bands

You can wrap thin cards around the print and then wrap it on a cardboard tube as in ① above. This method is for extremely fragile prints.

⑤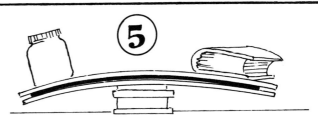

The print can be inserted between cards, as shown, and bent in the opposite direction of the curl by weights on both sides.

How a soda straw can be used to transfer liquid from one container to another

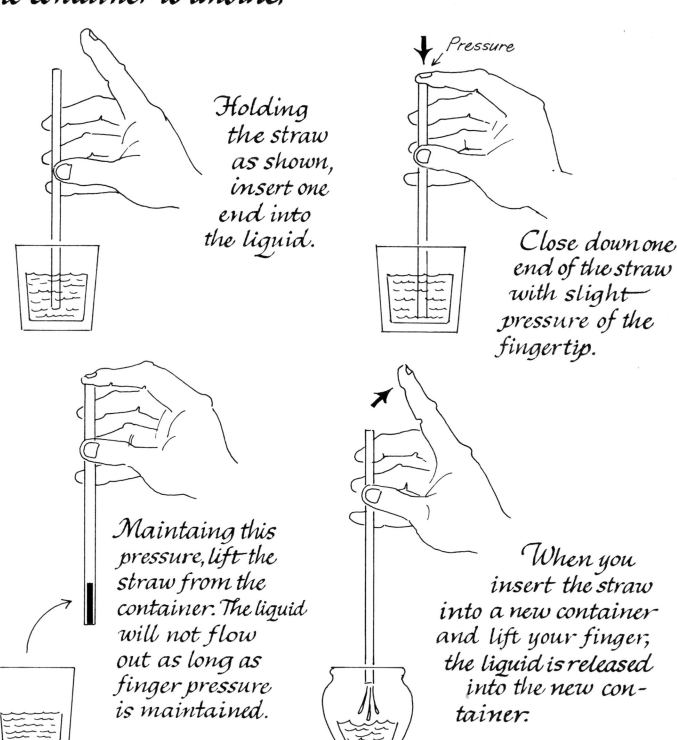

Holding the straw as shown, insert one end into the liquid.

Pressure

Close down one end of the straw with slight pressure of the fingertip.

Maintaing this pressure, lift the straw from the container. The liquid will not flow out as long as finger pressure is maintained.

When you insert the straw into a new container and lift your finger, the liquid is released into the new container.

How to prevent ink from spreading under tools

If you have trouble with ink spreading under your ruler, triangles, and T square when you use a ruling pen or other pens, adhere pieces of tape under the edge that you use. You can laminate several layers on top of one another if necessary. This lifts the tool away from the drawing surface and will prevent the ink from smudging the art work.

Triangle

Tape

Tape

T square

Ruler

How to use paste wax to help tools slide

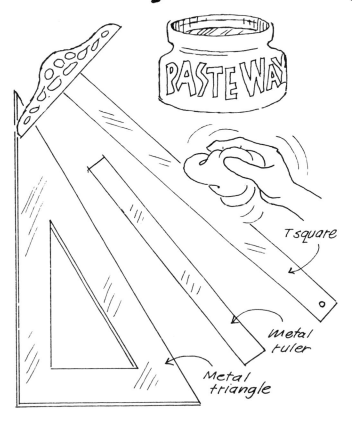

PASTE WAX

T square

Metal ruler

Metal triangle

If you want your tools to slide more easily, rub a light amount of paste wax on the under side and they will move easily over your drawing and board. Do not apply too much wax or it will have the opposite effect – make the tools sticky. Waxing is especially good for metal tools, but it may work on other materials. Sometimes a little wax on the sliding parts of a file drawer help the drawer slide more easily.

How to sharpen celluloid triangles

If edges of celluloid triangles get nicked and uneven, sharpen the edges as shown below and save triangles for much longer use.

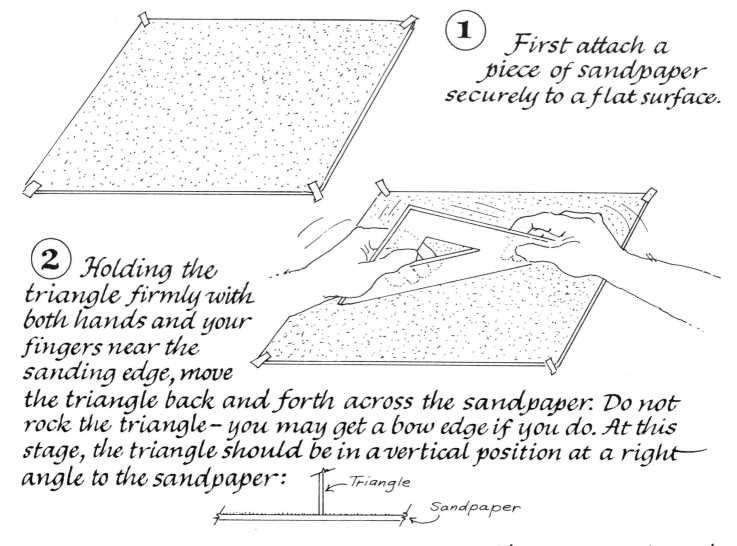

① First attach a piece of sandpaper securely to a flat surface.

② Holding the triangle firmly with both hands and your fingers near the sanding edge, move the triangle back and forth across the sandpaper. Do not rock the triangle – you may get a bow edge if you do. At this stage, the triangle should be in a vertical position at a right angle to the sandpaper:

Triangle

Sandpaper

③ Finally: Holding the triangle at a consistent angle, move it back and forth as before in order to sandpaper an edge on the side of the triangle.

Then reverse the angle and sandpaper again. You should get an edge similar to this.

Ways to get a deckle-edge effect on paper

Shown below are 5 different ways of creating a deckle-edge effect on paper.

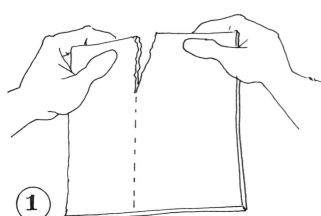

① *Carefully tear paper along a predetermined line.*

② *Hold a saw firmly against the edge and tear the paper, pulling against the saw.*

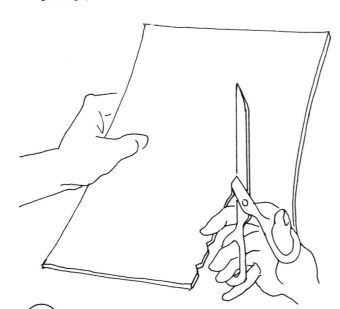

④ *Tear back and forth against a firmly held ruler.*

③ *With scissors, cut back and forth along a line.*

⑤ *Burn, here and there, and clean up. This gives the deckle edge an antique look as well.*

How to open stubborn jars and tubes

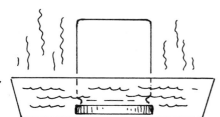

Soak the bottle upside down in hot water overnight.

Impossible tubes: Prick tube, use paint, and tape the hole when you're finished.

Hit the cap with light glancing taps in the direction of the unscrew.

Splash hot water on the bottle's neck.

Hold the cap at the tip of a flame from a match or lighter.

Use a small strip of sandpaper from your pencil pointer, wrap it around the jar's cap, and twist in both directions.

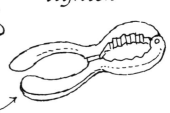

Regular pliers and nut or lobster crackers can be used.

How to maintain poster color or tempera

Once a month, remove all jar tops and add water. This will keep the paint from drying, so that it will always be ready for work.

An eye dropper is a handy tool for adding water

If the paint smells sour, add a drop or two of denatured alcohol.

If the paint dusts off the job when it is dry, add a drop or two of mucilage or glue to the jar.

If the paint is chalky, add a drop of glycerin to each jar. It will also slow down the drying time of the paint.

Gum arabic and oxgall can also be added to the paint if the paint does not adhere to the surface.

Making Your Own Tools

How to maintain a constant uncommon angle on art work

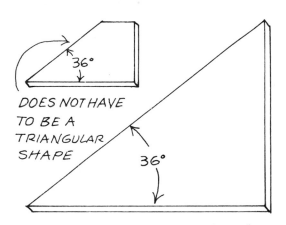

36°

DOES NOT HAVE TO BE A TRIANGULAR SHAPE

36°

If you have the problem of maintaining a constant uncommon angle in making a drawing, carefully measure and cut a triangle of the desired angle from a piece of illustration board. The edge can be smoothed with a piece of sandpaper.

This triangle can be moved across your T square in the same manner as a regular plastic or metal triangle and need not always be in a triangular shape.

How to make an aid for cropping photographs

First, cut 2 large L-shapes out of heavy paper or light cardboard. Use them on a photograph, or on a drawing, to find the best area of the photo to reproduce or use, as shown on the top of the next page.

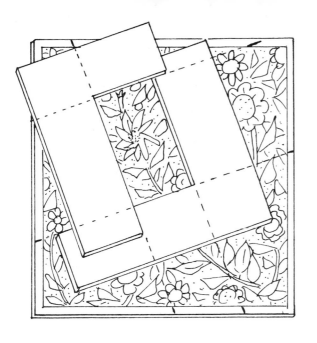

Move the 2 L-shaped cards around until you find the area of the photograph, or the drawing, you want to use. Once you establish the limits of the area, extend the sides to the edges of the photograph and mark for future use as shown with the dotted lines.

This method of using part of a picture is called "cropping."

How to make a device for drawing radiating lines

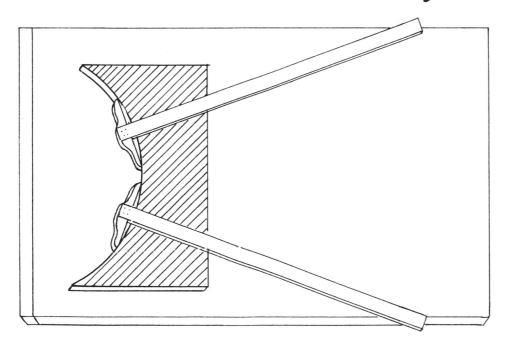

On a piece of heavy illustration board draw an arc of a large circle. Cut the piece of board out as shown at the left (shaded part), and secure it to the left side of the drawing board.

With the T square against the curve, touching it at the extremes of the head of the T square, draw radiating lines as desired. The arc can also be secured at the right side, the top, or at the bottom of the drawing board.

How to make a bridge from an old T square

Neck

Head

If you have an old, beat-up, wooden-headed, celluloid T square, measure off about a 12" section of the neck and cut it with a saw. (Pick a clean straight-edged section.)

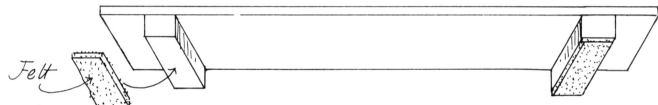

Felt

Glue small strips of wood (about ½" square) to either side. When they are dry, glue small pieces of felt to the strip bottoms to prevent scuffs and scratches.

Your hand rests on the bridge, which is over the art work, and does not touch the art. The straight edge of the bridge can be used for drawing straight lines. Do not make the bridge too long or it might belly down and touch the art work. A bridge can also be made from any smooth strip of wood.

How to make an inexpensive portable "light table"

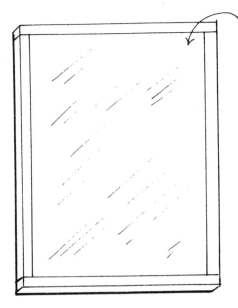

Buy a piece of heavy plate glass (18" x 24") from the local glazier. Have him smooth the edges. Then tape the edges well with adhesive or any other tape. Resting this glass on your

lap and a table edge, place a small lamp on the floor beneath the glass and use the glass as a light box. Flashlights or other battery lamps can also be used. To prevent eye strain, you can frost the glass, or have it done by a glazier.

How to make your own rubber stamp

Carefully remove the rubber from an old rubber stamp. First draw your new image on a piece of rubber or on a soft red rubber eraser and cut away the part you do not want to print. Glue this to the base of the old handle and use as desired. Remember when cutting the image that it must read in reverse so that it will print to read from left to right.

How to get a distorted effect by drawing on white rubber

A piece of white surgical rubber can be purchased in a surgical supply house.

Draw or letter a design on white rubber.

Pull and distort the rubber on a heavy board until you achieve the desired effect. Secure rubber shape well with tape. The board can be sent to the photostatter. The print you get back from him may need retouching because the edges of the images may become fuzzy due to stretching the rubber.

How to get texture effects with spray fixatives

One way to get texture effects, on rocks in a watercolor for example, is to paint the rocks, and, while the paint is still wet, to spray a fixative into the wet areas. Don't overdo it or you will lose the effect. And don't waste any time; work fast. Experiment many times on scrap paper before trying the technique on your art.

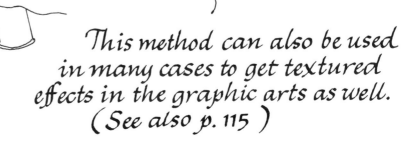

Mask

This method can also be used in many cases to get textured effects in the graphic arts as well.
(See also p. 115)

How to butt 2 pieces in an irregular joint

Suppose that you want to join two pieces of coloraid paper together in an irregular joint.

To begin with, rubber cement or paste down the first color on a board. ——

Mark the irregular joint before pasting the second color to the first color.

Carefully cut the joint through both papers, removing the unwanted part of the second color.

Carefully lift the second color sheet and remove the unwanted part of the first sheet so that lumps will not show. Reset the second color, and you should have a perfect mortise. ——

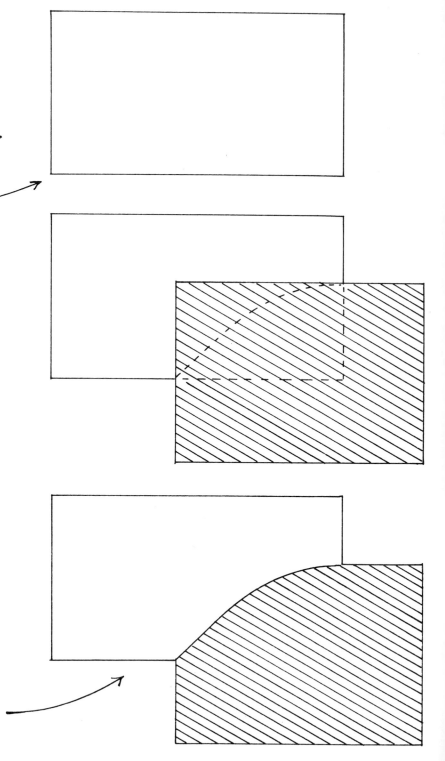

How to get an embossed effect with casein glue

Casein glue, mixed with water soluble color, can be used effectively to build up images for an embossed effect. When the mixture is dry, new layers of it can be added to build up the image until the desired embossed or raised effect has been achieved. Casein glue will adhere to acetate and most other art surfaces.

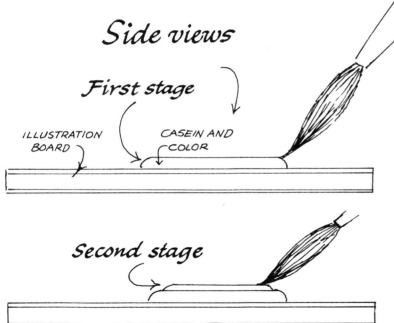

Side views

First stage

ILLUSTRATION BOARD

CASEIN AND COLOR

Second stage

Subsequent stages

The first application of mixed casein glue and paint should be carefully drawn because the edges of this first layer will be seen more than the subsequent layers, which will be smaller in area as you "terrace" the paint layer after layer.

The second application goes on top of the first application, and so on.

Continue "staging" until you get the effect you want.

How to use a wash-out technique in making a design

On illustration board paint a design with poster or tempera color.

When the design is dry, paint over the entire area as quickly as you can with waterproof ink.

After the ink has dried, wash the entire board under water. The original design will reappear in bright color and with an interesting quality to the line.

Using this technique with wax crayons and ink on rough mat board will produce a similar effect.

How to use transfer sheets and letters to achieve decorative effects

Transfer or pressure letters can be purchased in many sizes in most art stores. They come in outline — in black and white and sometimes in color.

There are also a variety of texture effects to be found in transfer sheets.

In order to apply a decorative pattern to a letter, first cut or press an outline letter where you want it ①. Then lay the pattern sheet over the letter ②. Carefully cut around the outline letter and burnish the entire letter ③. The design can then be photostatted larger or smaller as desired.

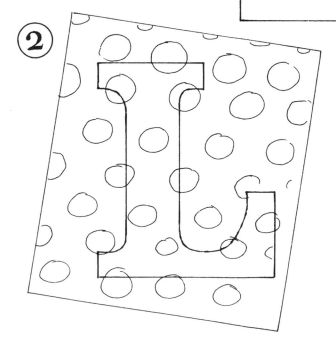

How to make a blue transfer sheet for pencil designs

Suppose you made a pencil drawing on a piece of tracing paper and now want to transfer the image to illustration board for making a final finished drawing. Instead of making a gray-pencil transfer sheet (the gray pencil lines are difficult to see), use a blue pastel for the sheet and you will then see the pencil lines more clearly as you trace the drawing.

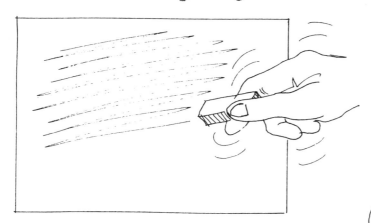

First, apply pastel to a separate tracing sheet. Then spread the ↗ pastel with rubber cement thinner and a small cotton ball. Repeat this procedure several times. Tape the drawing to the board and slip the blue transfer sheet, face down, between it and the board. <u>You will see the pencil lines of the drawing clearly.</u> Trace the drawing, transferring the image to the board. When you are finished, remove the tracing paper and also the drawing on top of the illustration board.

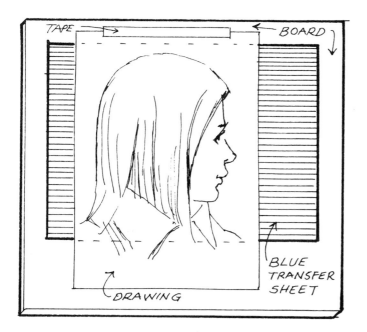

How to use an electric-drill sander as an eraser

Suppose you wanted to remove a section of a painted billboard, or a large painted name sign over a storefront, or a painted name on a directory in a public building or elsewhere. An electric drill with a sander attachment can be used to "erase" the unwanted part.

Just sand the unwanted area out carefully, clean it well, and repaint the new information as shown above and at left. A little retouching may be necessary.

Kinds of erasers and their uses

 **Soft pliable** rubber eraser is an all purpose eraser that cleans as it erases. It is the most common one used.

 **Kneaded eraser** for pencil, chalk, pastel and charcoal. It can be shaped to any convenient form and is nonabrasive. It is gray in color.

 **Ink eraser** is hard and abrasive. It will scratch out stubborn ink marks.

 Art gum eraser is free of grease and cannot scratch. It crumbles. It is used to remove pencil marks from inked art.

 **Plastic** (VINYL) drafting eraser for use on tracing cloth, film, or paper. It is hard and does not crumble.

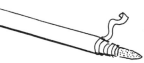 **Paper-wrapped** erasers are pencil shaped, soft or abrasive. For use in very small areas and can be pointed.

 **Dry, clean pad** eraser comes in a mesh bag with gum bits that sift through. It is used to clean large jobs such as signs and charts.

 Fiber glass eraser is cigar-shaped. Has a fiber-glass brush tip and is used for extremely difficult erasures.

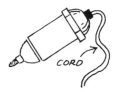 **Electric erasers** for general use. Move them gently in a rotating manner. Nibs are either soft or abrasive and are interchangeable.

CORD

Other kinds of "erasers"

Razor blades and knives can be used to remove heavy deposits of ink and paint. Use a gentle scraping motion. When you are near the surface of the paper, switch over to one of the other more conventional methods.

Cotton balls, Q-tips, swabs, and small pieces of clean rags can be used with rubber cement thinner to take grease, scuff marks, and other stubborn marks away. Use a gentle scrubbing action.

Erasing fluids (2 bottles — one a hypochlorite and the other an acid) can be applied successively on the mark and removed with a blotter.

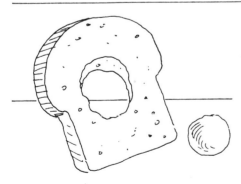

If there are no other erasers around, and you desperately need to erase some pencil smudges on a piece of art, take the center from a slice of any white wheat bread, roll it into a ball, and use it like you would an eraser. It really works.

Special abrasive powders are made for use in airbrushes for extremely difficult situations when all other erasing methods have failed.

How to erase

The most important thing to keep in mind when erasing is that you want to remove the spot completely — with the least possible damage if any to the surface of your drawing. After choosing the correct eraser, rub the spot gently in the actions shown below. Do not attack the surface roughly. The arrows show the directions in which the eraser moves. One should erase in many different directions, not just one.

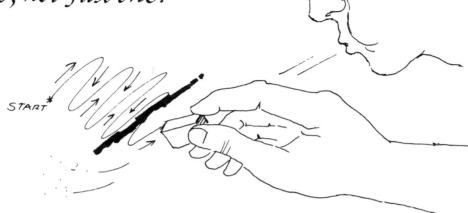

As you erase, blow the crumbs away. Otherwise you may grind dirty particles back into the surface.

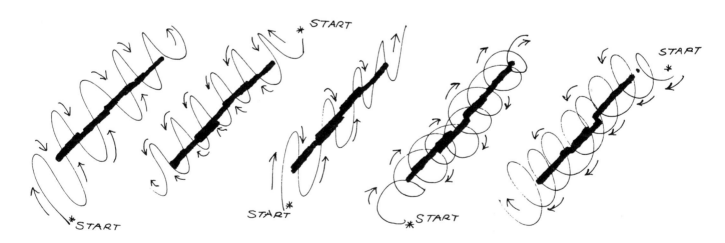

The diagrams show successive directions and the movement of the eraser and hand.

How to keep art you are working on clean

Always rest your hand on a piece of card, or a blotter, when you are working on finished art. Use the left hand to hold the blotter in place. Be careful not to move the card over wet art work.

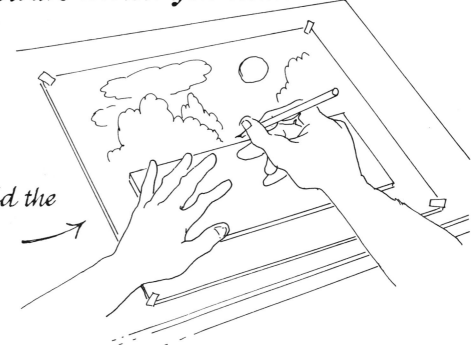

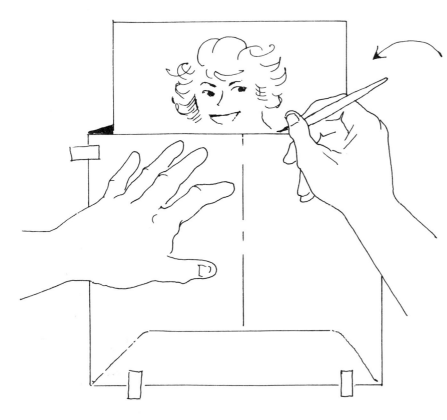

Cut the top from and tape a large clean envelope to your drawing board and put the drawing inside. The drawing has already been sketched out and you are now going to apply the ink or other medium. Slip the sketch out as you proceed with the inking. Your hand will rest on the envelope and the drawing will stay clean. You can make your own envelope with thin cards and tape.

How to clean a mat

There may be an occasion when you want to clean a soiled mat. First lay the mat flat on a clean level surface. Dust with a clean cloth or a brush to remove all loose particles and then rub it with a soft kneaded eraser. An abrasive ink eraser, used gently, and sharp stencil knives and eraser may remove stubborn spots, but you must be careful never to damage the surface. Also try clean rags and rubber cement thinner, gently rubbed over and over the mat. Finally, if necessary, use lacquer thinner with cotton balls, to clean the mat completely.

<u>Cleaning agents</u> →

INK ERASER

RUBBER CEMENT THINNERS

LACQUER THINNER

KNEADED ERASER

COTTON BALLS

Q-TIP

How to clean off stubborn rubber cement smudges

Any one, or all, of the above suggestions for cleaning a mat can also be used to clean stubborn smudges from a completed mechanical. Try not to damage the surface, but if you do, dab light touches of white retouch paint to the scuffed areas with the aid of a cotton ball or a small piece of sponge. The mechanical, too, should lie flat on a clean level surface.

WHITE

How to use strips of blotters for "mopping up"

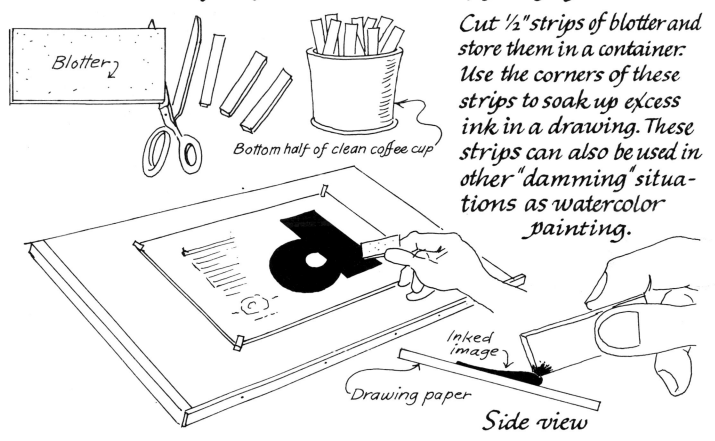

Blotter

Bottom half of clean coffee cup

Cut ½" strips of blotter and store them in a container. Use the corners of these strips to soak up excess ink in a drawing. These strips can also be used in other "damming" situations as watercolor painting.

Inked image

Drawing paper

Side view

How to keep a water jar clean

It's a good idea to add a few drops of a mild detergent to your water jar whenever you change the water. It will not affect the use of the water in most cases, but it will enable you to keep a clean jar, and also make the cleaning of the jar much easier.

How to keep clean hands in messy situations

If it is necessary to use your hands in messy situations — as in silk-screen printing, when rubber gloves are not used — first wash your hands in warm water with soap that will give lots of suds. Remove your hands with suds from the water, and rub the hands together until all suds disappear. Dry rub the suds into your hands. Then scratch the soap bar with your fingernails, getting some soap under the nails, and proceed to work. When you are finished and wash your hands in warm water you will find they become clean easily — and under the fingernails, too.

How to prevent things from sticking to your hands in hot weather

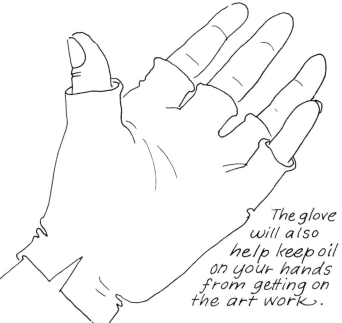

The glove will also help keep oil on your hands from getting on the art work.

If you have a problem due to excessively sweaty hands and hot, humid working conditions, purchase a pair of white cotton gloves (undertaker's gloves are good) and cut the fingers off the glove. Wearing the remaining glove part will eliminate this problem. The glove will not interfere with the normal movement of your fingers.

How to clean up lines in a black-ink drawing

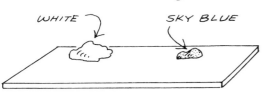

If you mix a little blue water-color with your opaque white touch-up, it will make your touch-up/clean-up/retouching of ink line art much easier because you will be able to see it. And the light blue will be so light that it will not reproduce when you send the line art to the printer or the engraver.

How to use the back of your hand as a paperweight

Since the back of your hand perspires less and is generally cleaner than your palm side, try and develop the habit of using it for holding down your paper, or other work, as you draw with the other hand.

Rubber Cement

How to "make" a rubber-cement thinner dispenser

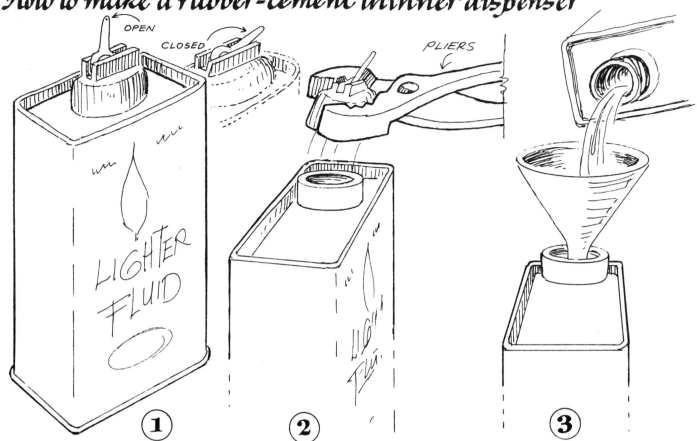

An empty lighter fluid can makes an excellent rubber cement dispenser ①. When it is empty, you can easily remove the top by gently twisting and turning it with the aid of pliers ②. A small funnel can be used to fill it from the large gallon thinner container ③.

The spout on the lighter fluid can simply flips down to seal the can closed when you are not using it.

An oil can is another inexpensive rubber cement thinner dispenser that you can buy in any hardware store.

After removing the spout, the can is filled as in ③ above.

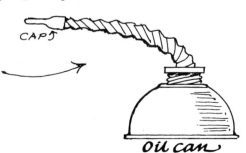

What to do if you spill rubber cement

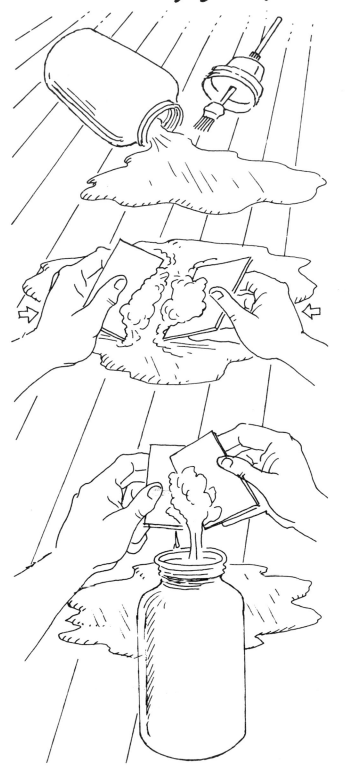

If rubber cement is spilled, act fast. First "right" the container and stand it away from the action.

With two small stiff cards, start gathering the cement as shown. If it was spilled on a clean surface, return the recovered cement to the container. Repeat until all cement is saved or cleaned from the floor.

If cement is spilled on a dirty area, place the picked-up cement into a coffee container (or on a piece of newspaper) and deposit it in a trash can.

Dry cement on the floor can also be picked up with a rubber cement pick-up.

Work fast !!!

Keep a supply of small stiff cards (3" x 5" approximately) always handy.

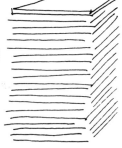

How rubber cement can keep a drawing clean

Sometimes, when you are drawing on a board, you will want to keep one special area as clean as possible.

Rubber cement can be used for this purpose. Coat the area you're concerned about with it.

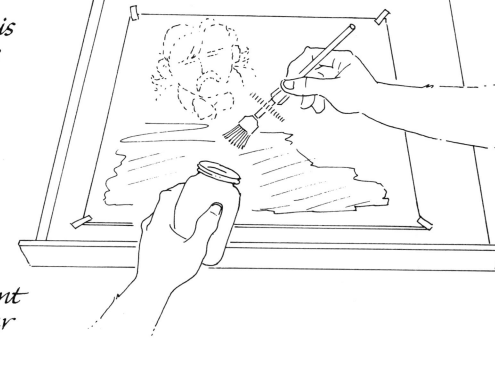

When the cement is dry, make your drawing in the area not covered by the rubber cement and when that part is dry and finished, remove the rubber cement with a pick-up.
You will find that the area is perfectly clean.

How to prevent rubber cement stains on silkscreened paper

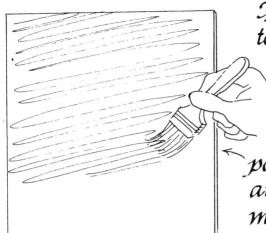

If you have many items to adhere to a colored silk screened paper, brush rubber cement over the entire area of the screened paper. After it dries and the items are dry-mounted down, the cement can be picked

up, leaving no visible stain marks. But if you "spot-cement," the excess cement beyond the limits of the images may leave a stain. The 3 steps below show how to avoid this.

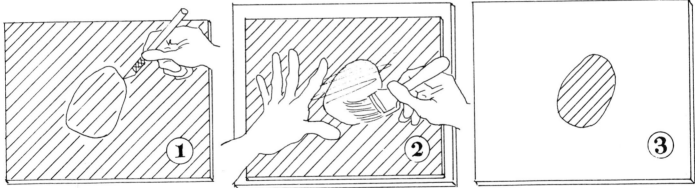

First cut out the shape to be adhered to the screened paper ①. Save the paper left over and use it as a mask to be positioned on the screened paper exactly where you want it ②. Holding the mask against the screened paper, carefully brush rubber cement into the open area ②. Be sure that no rubber cement creeps under the edges. Hold the mask in position until the cement is dry and then remove it. Rubber cement the back of the shape and when it is dry, carefully match its edges with the edges of the rubber cemented area on the screened paper and press. There should be no stains ③.

Spraying and Fixative
How to use an aerosol spray can

First carefully read all of the instructions and directions on the can. Some of these are repeated here for emphasis.

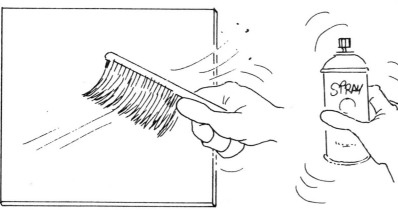

Be sure the surface to be sprayed is clean.

Shake the can well before use.

Test the spray on scrap to be sure it works well.

Always keep the top on when not in use.

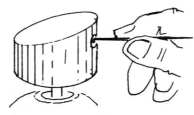

Use a needlepoint to reopen if the spray hole gets jammed.

A light spray will waterproof paper cups.

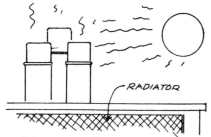

RADIATOR

Never store cans on a heated surface — they may burst.

Use a moist hanky when using spray a great deal.

If you must remove spray fixative from art, try some lacquer thinner and a rag or a cotton ball— carefully.

LACQUER THINNER

How to use fixative to prevent tape from pulling up the surface of your working card

If you use a card cover on your drawing board as a working surface, you will find that when you remove art work which has been <u>taped</u> down, the tape will leave scuff marks.

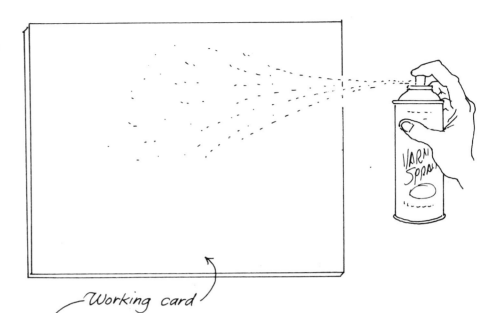

Working card

Art

Tape

Enlarged view of corner

ART
SCUFFS

To avoid this, spray the card cover first with acrylic spray coating fixative; then when you pick up the tape, it will not tear the surface.

As you change cover cards from time to time, spray them generously as shown above so that this (see circle) will not happen to your cover.

How to use a toothbrush or atomizer for spray effects

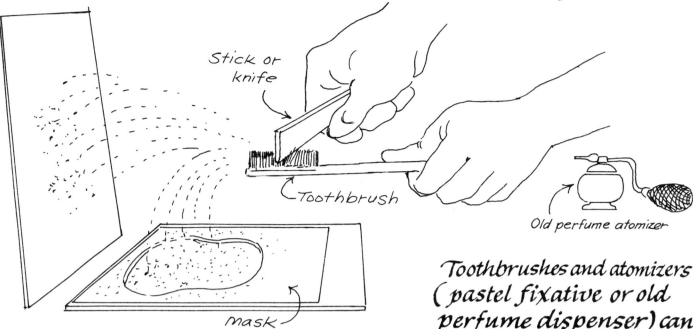

Stick or knife

Toothbrush

Old perfume atomizer

Mask

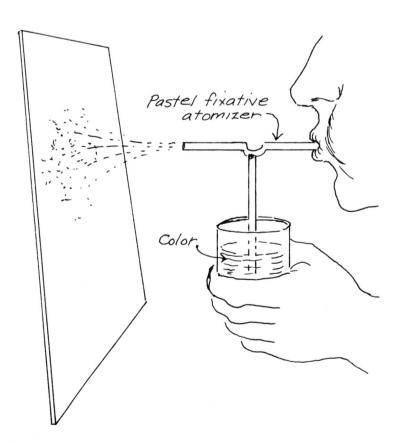

Pastel fixative atomizer

Color

Toothbrushes and atomizers (pastel fixative or old perfume dispenser) can both be used as effective spraying devices. At left, use of the toothbrush is shown. Dip the brush in paint and use a knife or small stick to spatter the art.

Next, the use of an atomizer with thin color (ink, watercolor, and other media) to achieve spray effects is shown.

Practice with different solutions.

How spray fixative can be used in making a design

There may be an occasion when a subtle value change is required in a design. The design to the left ① is an example. The sky is light red and the hills are the only other image. You want a subtle value change in the sky to suggest a sun. You can do this by cutting a circular stencil, or mask, and using spray fixative. First cut a mask or stencil of a circle for the sun as in ②. Position this mask over your design and spray it with fixative as in ③. The result will be a faint suggestion of a sun in the red sky as in ④.

Dulling spray can be used on shiny metallic surfaces in a similar manner.

When sprayed on coloraid paper a regular spray fixative will give a clouded tint effect.

When workable fixative is sprayed on any surface, you can easily paint with watercolor over the area.

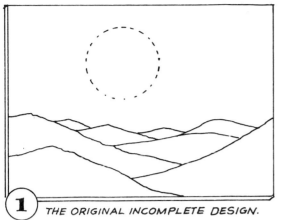

① THE ORIGINAL INCOMPLETE DESIGN. THE DOTTED CIRCLE IS THE SUN'S POSITION FOR SPRAYING WITH FIXATIVE.

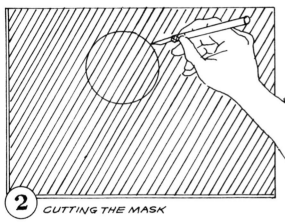

② CUTTING THE MASK

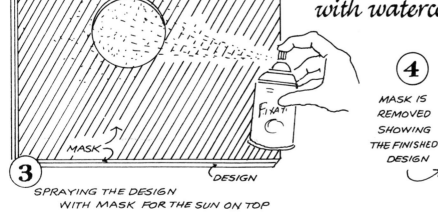

③ SPRAYING THE DESIGN WITH MASK FOR THE SUN ON TOP

MASK

DESIGN

FIXATIVE

④ MASK IS REMOVED SHOWING THE FINISHED DESIGN

How to draw guide lines on your drawing board for checking and drawing rectangles

Most artists attach a thin white card or illustration board to their drawing board as a working surface that can be changed from time to time.

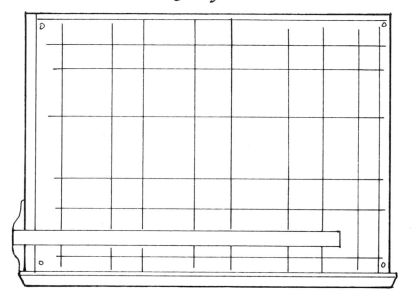

Thin ink lines forming rectangles of various sizes can be measured and marked unobtrusively on the card or board and used to check rectangles of layouts and the trueness or the "squareness" of photographs and other art.

If you have many cards of the same size on which borders are to be drawn, all exactly the same distance from the cards' edges, first draw corresponding marks on a clean drawing surface. Tape the cards, matching the marks, and rule in the borders with a pencil or pen. Remove the card and tape the next one and repeat the same method. This way will save time because no ruler is needed for measuring.

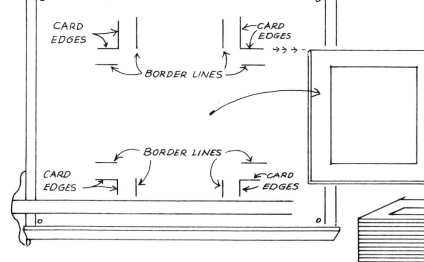

CARD EDGES

CARD EDGES

BORDER LINES

BORDER LINES

CARD EDGES

CARD EDGES

How to make a guide for slanted parallel elements

1 Tape a sheet of acetate (or thin card or other material) on your drawing board and draw parallel ink lines. ➔

ACETATE

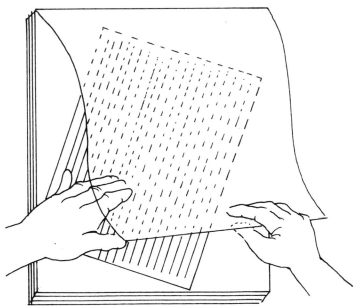

2 Slip the acetate guide under the tracing paper at the desired angle. Tape the guide so that it will not move.

3 Following the parallel lines under the tracing paper, develop your design, as with the lettering above.

Timothy

How to make a template for dotted lines

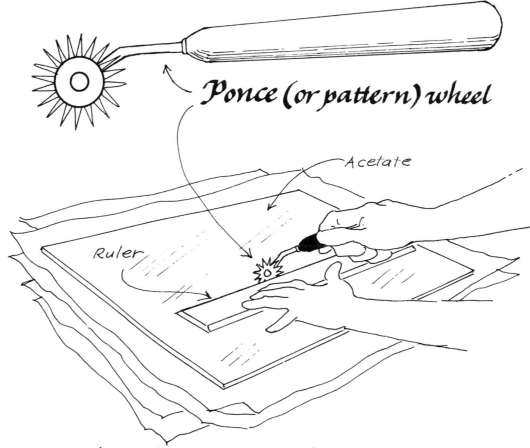

Ponce (or pattern) wheel

Acetate

Ruler

Lay a straight edge on a small piece of heavy acetate. The acetate rests on a soft backing like a large blotter or a folded newspaper. Rule a line of holes with the ponce wheel, impressing the regularly spaced holes into the acetate. Turn the acetate over and sandpaper the holes.

The template can now be used, with a wad of color, to make dotted lines on art or anywhere else.

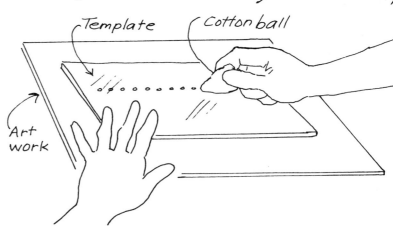

Template Cotton ball

Art work

How to make a template for repeated patterns

If you have to draw many duplicate designs — such as lettering signs — cut a template as shown.

Knife

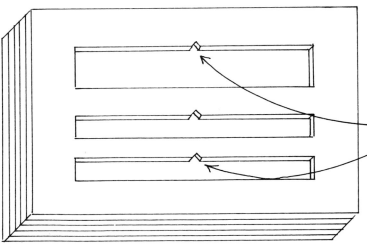

First make your layout and cut out rectangles for guide lines on all copies.

Nicks can be cut in the slots to show the center line.

Using the same procedure, you can make templates for all sorts of other designs.

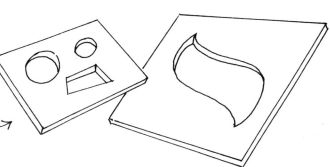

How to make an oval template

After cutting an oval out of a stiff card sand the edges of the oval with a small piece of sandpaper.

Smooth the curve but...

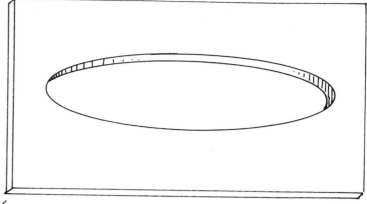

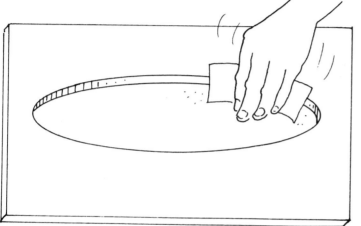

...don't overdo it or you may distort the curve.

Spray front and back with varnish spray to protect the template.

Build up the under-neath part with small strips of cardboard or tape so that when you use ink, the ink will not blot.

If you use a technical pen, be sure to hold the pen in a vertical position against the edge of the oval.

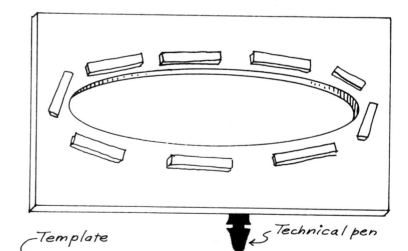

Artwork Template Technical pen

Section through side view

How to make a template for repeated curves

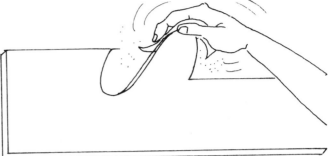

Suppose you want to make a border like this

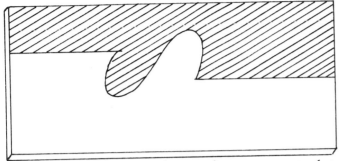

On heavy card with a straight edge bottom, design a curve and cut it out with a mat knife.

Discard the shaded part. Sand-paper the edges to smooth the curve.

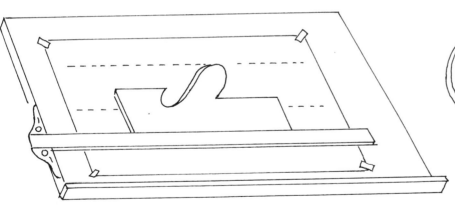

Draw guide lines (see dotted lines above) and space the curves as desired. With a technical pen draw repeats of the curve. Use the template against your T square as you would a regular triangle.

All kinds of variations are possible with this method.

Proportional Aids
How to make a proportional scaling device

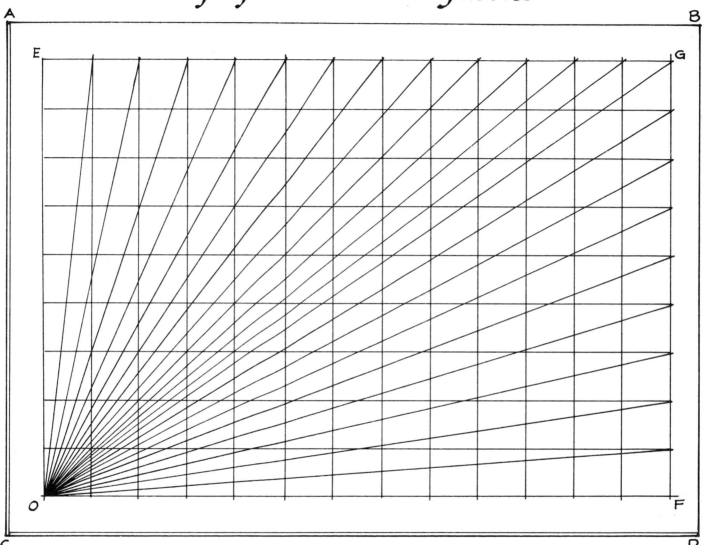

On a piece of acetate (ABCD), draw the left-hand vertical line, OE, and at a right angle to it draw the horizontal line, OF. Divide these lines into any equal number of equal dimensions and draw the grid, OFGE. From O, construct diagonals to these outside points and draw the radiating lines. By laying this device over a small rectangle, you can mark off any enlargement desired. It can also be used for making reductions.

How to enlarge elements on a design proportionately

Design to be enlarged.

With T square and triangles, extend the design's limits to the <u>edges</u> of the design and establish points A, B, C, and D. →

Begin to enlarge the design by drawing a diagonal from corner 0 and establishing O' on the design at the bottom. With 0 as the radiating point, extend and draw lines OA to OA', OB to OB', OC to OC' and OD to OD'. From points A' and B' draw parallel lines across the new design, and from points C' and D' erect perpendicular lines. As these lines intersect, they form the enlarged rectangle, which is in exact proportion to the smaller design at top left of this page.

Limits of an irregular area can be extended proportionally in a similar fashion.

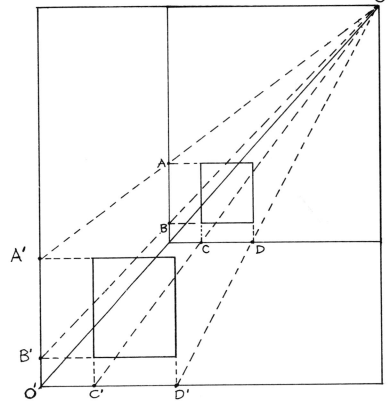

Metric Equivalents for Easy Reference

Linear Measures

1 centimeter	0.3937 inch
1 inch	2.54 centimeters
1 decimeter	3.937 inches, 0.328 foot
1 foot	3.048 decimeters
1 meter	39.37 inches, 1.09.36 yards
1 yard	0.9144 meter
1 decameter	1.9884 rods
1 rod	0.5029 decameter
1 kilometer	0.621.37 mile
1 mile	1.609.3 kilometers

Square Measures

1 sq. centimeter	0.1550 sq. inch
1 sq. inch	6.452 sq. centimeters
1 sq. decimeter	0.1076 sq. foot
1 sq. foot	9.2903 sq. decimeters
1 sq. meter	1.196 sq. yards
1 sq. yard	0.8361 sq. meter
1 acre	160 sq. rods
1 sq. rod	0.00625 acre
1 hectare	2.47 acres
1 acre	0.4047 hectare
1 sq. kilometer	0.386 sq. mile
1 sq. mile	2.59 sq. kilometers

Measures of Volume

1 cu. centimeter	0.061 cu. inch
1 cu. inch	16.39 cu. centimeters
1 cu. decimeter	0.0353 cu. foot
1 cu. foot	28.317 cu. decimeters
1 cu. yard	0.7646 cu. meter
1 stere	0.2759 cord
1 cord	3.624 steres
1 liter	0.908 qt. dry, 1.0567 qts. liq.
1 qt. dry	1.101 liters
1 qt. liquid	0.9463 liter
1 decaliter	2.6417 gals., 1.135 pecks
1 gal.	0.3785 decaliter
1 peck	0.881 decaliter
1 hectoliter	2.8375 bushels
1 bushel	0.3524 hectoliter

Weights

1 gram	0.03527 ounce
1 ounce	28.35 grams
1 kilogram	2.2046 pounds
1 pound	0.4536 kilogram
1 metric ton	0.98421 English ton
1 English ton	1.016 metric tons

Circle Formulas
How to find parts of circles and globes

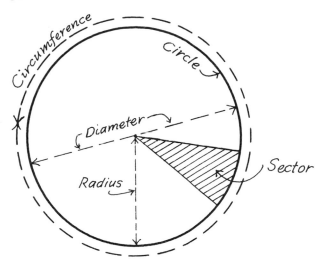

All circles have 360°

Formulas

To find the _diameter_ of a circle, multiply the circumference by .31831

To find the _circumference_ of a circle, multiply the diameter by 3.1416

To find the _area_ of a circle, multiply the square of the diameter by .7854

To find the _surface_ of a ball, multiply the square of the diameter by 3.1416

Suppose you have a circle and a square both of which have the same known area. You want to know the length of a side of the square. You find this by dividing the area of either the circle or the square by .8862.

To find the _cubic volume_ in a ball, multiply the cube of the diameter by .5236
The cube is the diameter x the diameter x the diameter.

To find the _area of a sector,_ use the following formula:

$$\text{Area of sector} = \frac{\substack{\text{angle of the sides}\\ \text{of the sector (radii)}}}{360} \times \text{the area of the circle}$$

Note where the decimal points are in each case shown above.

Picture-Frame Sizes
How to plan picture and frame sizes

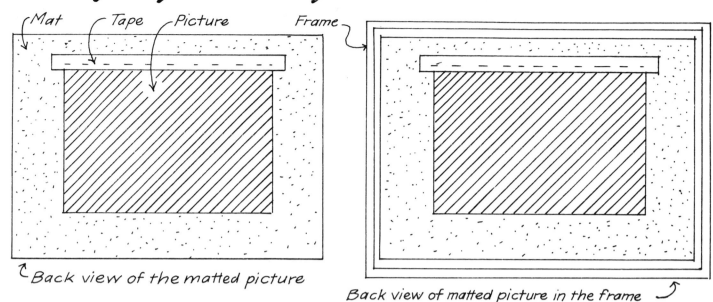

Mat — Tape — Picture — Frame

Back view of the matted picture

Back view of matted picture in the frame

When frame sizes are given, the size refers to the matted picture which fits the back of the frame, not the actual size of the frame. Standard frame (picture) sizes are listed below. Special frames can be made to order:

5" x 7"	8"×10"	9"×12"	10"×14"
11"×14"	12"×16"	14"×18"	16"×20"
18"×24"	20"×24"	22"×28"	24"×30"
24"×36"			

Until you have the facilities for making your own frames, it would be well to limit your framable pictures to these sizes.

Different kinds of printing papers

In order of increasing smoothness, the finishes of paper are: antique, eggshell, vellum, machine finish (MF), and English finish* (EF). Additional smoothness is obtained by super calendering (SC). Some finishes, such as linen, tweed, pebble, and cloud, are embossed as the paper leaves the machine. Characteristics of printing paper for the designer to consider are the grain (fiber direction) for folding, basic weight, strength, print quality, color, brightness, opacity, gloss, and refractiveness. * smoothly calendered book paper

Kinds of printing papers, their uses and sizes

__Bond__ paper is commonly used for letters. It accepts ink readily, is easily erased, and usually comes in 8½" x 11" size sheets.

__Coated__ paper refers to a regular paper that has been given a smooth, glossy coating. It is used when high printing quality is desired. (25"x38")

__Text__ papers come in interesting textures and colors. They are used for special announcements, booklets, and brochures. (25"x 38")

__Cover__ papers are coated text papers in heavier weights and matching colors. They are used for booklet covers primarily. (20"x 26")

__Book__ paper is used for trade and text books and comes with antique or smooth finish. It is less expensive than text papers. (25"x38")

__Offset__ paper is similar to coated and uncoated book paper. It is made primarily for offset lithography printing. (25"x 38")

__Index__ paper is stiff and receives writing ink easily. It comes in smooth and antique finishes and is inexpensive. (22½"x 35" and 25½"x30½")

__Newsprint__ paper, used for newspapers, is also inexpensive. It is very absorbent. (24"x 36)

__Tag__* paper is tinted on one or both sides. It has good bend quality and with a surface good for practically all purposes. (24"x 36) * US term

If you have a question about paper, ask your production department or call your local paper dealer.

INDEX